Foreword

I'm writing this book simply as a musician that's sick of seeing amazing artists get taken advantage of, especially while they're starting out. I've read so many of the music business books and taken a lot of courses. I've learned by trial and error what works and what doesn't work. I've spent money on the bullshit and I took the road of "hard-knocks" to hopefully save you from doing the same. I'll be the first to admit I'm still constantly learning, every single day. In the same way I look back on what I was doing 5 years ago and think, "what the hell was I thinking"...I'm sure I'll do the same 5 years from now when I read this book. That's learning, that's growing. By the simple fact that you're reading this I know you're the type of person that strives to do the same.

When writing this book I didn't want to just give general concepts on what to do, I wanted to give you a real blueprint wherever I could. You'll see this book is full of step-by-step instructions in an easy-to-read format. Through this book I'll give you websites to use, free apps you can download, how to make the most out of a limited budget and how best to use your budget as it grows. Most of all, I want to teach you how to grow your career the right way. The problem I've found with a lot of the educational books or blogs out there is that in the end they're trying to sell you something. I've read so many books where the end goal is not for you to be successful on your own, it's to bring you into their "master class" where they can teach you more for a fee. You've probably read tons of blog posts that look real until the end when they want you to *sign up for their music promotion service for only $25 a month.*

Music is an outlet for me, I'm passionate about keeping musicians safe from the scoundrels surrounding the music industry. I've played now for about 25 years and studied jazz piano as well as guitar. I've managed bookings, crowd-funding campaigns, marketing, social media, created low and high-budget music videos, kept track of finances and budgets, booked full tours, album production, mixing…well pretty much all the things you can do starting out as a musician nowadays. Have I made it yet? No, not by my own standards I haven't. I'm still pushing the boulder up the mountain just like you - I know what we're up against right now very well, I know the limited tools we have right now to overcome them.

When I left college I went into the world of Investment Banking, specifically business financing. Although I moved up quickly to partner in a successful firm, I hated what I did and felt like I was adding to a lot of the problems in the world. But in that time I learned a lot about business. That business knowledge is crucial and has saved me more times than I can count through my music career. I'm part of a unique subset of the millennial generation that was around before social media existed. Facebook blew up my sophomore year of college which left me in a unique place to study and understand how social media works and how to maximize its potential but not lose the sense of in-person, real-world connections that are needed (especially in the music business) to form relationships that last.

Whether you're a solo artist, a band, a DJ or any other form of music entertainer you can use the steps in this book to grow your career into a stable and lasting one. The steps used in this book are also scalable, meaning that if you have 20 fans or 20,000 you can build off of these growth techniques to continue getting more fans, lowering costs associated with being in a band and make more income while doing it.

Chapter - 1 Mindset

"In the music business bigger is not necessarily better. In fact, I believe smaller is actually better." Chuck Kaye, Dreamworks, SBK Publishing

Every music industry book I've read starts out by telling you that if you're expecting to become the next Taylor Swift, Led Zeppelin or Beatles that you're in the wrong place. I've read almost all of them and trust me, they all start out with something like *keep a level head and be practical and you can make a solid living playing music...but don't chase after arena shows and huge fame because the odds are the same as winning the lotto.*

We'll I would like to start by saying the opposite. If becoming the next Led Zeppelin is your goal in music than that is exactly what you will achieve and this book is a tool you will use as part of the journey. Maybe your goal isn't to play massive arena shows, maybe it's to have a song on the radio or to play at Coachella. Whatever that is, hold on to it – it's the most important piece of your music career. That goal is the reason you practice and write so many songs, the reason you spend countless hours replying to fans, run Twitter follow campaigns, email campaigns and endlessly hunt for new ways to connect your music with people.

I don't want to spend too much time on mindset in this book and want to focus on real practical things you need to do but without a firm and true goal it's like rowing a boat out into the ocean and not having a destination to paddle towards. You might as well just be paddling in circles because you don't know where you need to go. The same is true in life with goals, once you figure out what you truly want to do it makes it much easier to actually figure out how to get there. So don't forget about that dream and don't leave it vague. In fact you should take that dream and set a date you would like to do it by. If your goal is to play the main stage at Coachella figure out what year you want to do that. Choose a practical time-frame, if you haven't stepped onto any stage yet sorry to burst your bubble but it won't be happening this year. *Lorde being the loose exception to that statement.* Choose a time frame that makes sense for that goal, maybe it's in five years. What you've just done is turn that long turn "dream" into a "goal". Now you can start to work back from there on the things you'll need to do to reach that goal. How many fans will you need by then? Write that down. How many do you need to gain to get there? Write that down. How many per year, per month and per week do you need to reach? How can you measure your progress every single day? That's how you should think about your goals.

The next thing you need to understand is that it's not going to happen overnight. Have you ever heard anybody say it's not the destination that matters, it's the journey. Being a musician is a constant journey and you must remember to enjoy every step of it because it only gets better the more you work at it. It's just like when you first learned to start playing your instrument; if you're just starting out in the music business it's tough – just like practice can be. Getting gigs won't be as easy, the press will not want to write about you, recording might just seem like a distant dream. But just like learning how to play your instrument, it gets better. Each small break makes it easier for you to keep growing and you learn to appreciate when it was tough and the local bar down the street was the biggest gig you got. Stick with it, that's the point. The only way to fail at this (besides not knowing how to play) is to quit. I repeat, the only way to fail is to quit...don't quit!

Next up, the big break...you're not going to get it. That's right, you are not going to get that big break you've been waiting for. The music industry isn't American Idol despite claims by network television...the true breaks that happen are the small to medium sized breaks you create for yourself. That record label isn't going to gamble $100,000 on your garage recordings and 100 person local shows. You favorite band isn't going to stumble into a bar, hear your sound and bring your band on a world tour with them. A millionaire isn't going to walk up to you...well you get the point, right? Does it happen? Yes, people are discovered on YouTube, label execs have signed bands out of a bar and Toni Braxton caught her big break singing to herself at an Amoco station while pumping gas. But that's not the norm...those are beautiful stories and definitely help to sell records, but the majority of you will have to work hard for it. It's a hill, and you have to climb it...there are no elevators to the top. Again, respect the journey.

That leads me to running a business:

"I just want to play music, fuck everything else" – old musicians proverb

Whether you're a band, a solo artist or anything else in the music industry you need to understand you're a business. You need to consider yourself 50% business entrepreneur and 50% artist. As you grow you might consider getting other people to handle mundane tasks, bookings, tour planning, marketing, merch, websites, etc. but until then you're going to be handling it all. And you should respect that and learn as much of it as you can, because without some knowledge of this you won't be able to teach others to do this or maintain control as you hand these tasks off. A great book about growing any business: "E-Myth Revisited – Why Most Small Businesses Don't Work and What to Do About It" by Michael Gerber; this is a great business education book on how to grow your business correctly while handing off roles you used to do yourself to others that will be working for you.

Finally, and then I promise I'm done with the mindset BS – respect your fans, they are your life-line and your oxygen. Connect with them every chance you get. You don't need to act like you're too big for them. Be real with them, treat them with the respect they deserve and it will go a long way. Remember, without them you have no music career.

Chapter 2 - Research and Getting Started

"We cannot do everything at once but we can do something at once." - Calvin Coolidge

Find Your Sound. First thing's first, you need to know what your sound is. You probably have an idea of your sound but here's what I mean:

1. What is your genre?
2. Who are three mainstream artists you sound like

You should have a fast answer for both of these questions you can recite to anybody on the fly. I would suggest keeping your genre similar across the board for what you're doing. Don't be a group that plays country songs sometimes and hardcore punk rock other times with rap mixed in between - *I mean, unless you're making that work somehow.* Also spend some serious time being able to find the artists that you sound most like. This will help you in a lot of ways but the simplest is that people identify with those big artists more than they will with a genre. Blues-rock doesn't sound as appealing as telling somebody, "we sound like Black Keys mixed with Jack White". Get it?

If you are just getting started I would suggest really spending some time to find this sound, don't just jump right into your music career without shaping and crafting what your sound will be. If you're a band you'll want to get together to practice and do some writing together. Don't just take whatever song the lead singer wrote 5 years ago, see what comes out when you all play together and work off that. Really find what excites you and try to hone in on it - again, if you think as a business you wouldn't just open a coffee shop + sushi restaurant + gas station mixed together to appeal to everybody that you think wants to visit, you would find what you're best at and hone in on that.

Next thing to do is market research (boring right), you need to define your target audience. What age group are they? Are they mainly female, male or both? Where do they listen to music? What kind of social platforms are they primarily on? It is Facebook and Twitter or Snapchat and Instagram? Can they go into bars, do they like festivals? What would they most like out of an artist and what do they not appreciate? Where do they find music and how do they discover new artists?

One of my early "bands" was actually an a cappella group I was in when I was about 17. We would get hired for sweet sixteen parties, backyard events and other stage showcases around Chicago. One of our first big shows was for about 4000 people in a gymnasium for a rally. We decided to open up with an a cappella version of Ludacris' "Rollout". The looks on their faces as the five of us did our this a cappella rendition of Rollout is something I won't forget. We jumped genres and didn't think of the fans and what they would want to hear - it was one of those moments you finish the song and people are not sure if they should clap or not because they were so confused. I made the mistake once more playing years later in an indie-rock band outside an Oktoberfest party, we thought because it was Oktoberfest people would appreciate a polka song. One girl who had come to three previous shows starting actually booing us during the song. The point is, this stuff is important...know who your fans are, know what they want and be consistent.

Also when you figure this out think about your look & feel and most importantly, your story. It's sadly more important than the diminished chord that resolves to the root in 5/8 time during the bridge. Here's how you should think about your story, if you've ever watched The Voice or American Idol the first thing you notice is that the show is about]25% actual singing or performances and 75% segments about the artist and their life. As a musician, this is one of the many reasons I can't tune in and watch these shows. As a businessman I find it amazing that they dedicate this much time to the story over the actual performance when the entire show is based around watching people sing. It's because the average fan of music relates more to the story about the artist first and then the music. Is that how you discover music? Maybe and maybe not, you're probably not the average music fan though - you're a musician. Finding your story and what makes you important will be the first thing people grasp onto.

Along with the look, feel and story comes your bio, your name (if you're a band or play under a different title), clothing you'll wear and what your videos or photoshoots will be like. This all plays into what I'll call your brand – it's what people think of when they think of you. Are you edgy and rocker, an upscale jazz musician, a rapper? Your style will define your brand and who you are. The brand is what will sell everything, it's what will grow your music, it's what blogs will write about when they write about you, it's what your fans will ultimately love about you. Which brings me to a next very important point.

Your music isn't actually your product. Maybe twenty years ago music was, but not in the new music industry. If you haven't come to terms with that please take a second to collect yourself and then read on. Deep breath, okay. You need to stop thinking of your music as the product you sell. Will you sell signed hard-copy CDs at your shows? Yes, you'll sell a lot and it will be a big part of your income stream. Are vinyl sales up right now? Yes, but not nearly where they were when it was the only way to listen to music. Your CDs and vinyl are merch and you can sell them at shows and on your website but your actual music needs to be available everywhere to be listened to for free. I told you I wrote this book to be direct, to the point and to simply tell you what to do. I'm not going to go into all research for this statement or how labels fucked up so badly for so many years trying to fight this trend - just trust me that a lot of consideration has gone into this statement: stop trying to charge people money to hear your music. Your music is marketing material, you will use your music to get fans into you or your band and to connect with them. As a musician it's the strongest piece of marketing content you have so use your music every way you can to get more people into you, but stop thinking of it as the product you sell.

So if your music is just marketing material what is your actual product? Your product is every way you make money as a band...don't worry, I'll go into way more detail on all of this but that could include: ticket sales, crowd-funding, patreon support, donations, merchandise sales, licensing deals, private events and yes even your tip jar!

So I said I was not going to talk too much about general theory so I want to dive right into this...getting started I needed to at least lay a foundation with those few points so we could be on the same page as you read the rest of this book.

Chapter 3 – Creating Music and Recording It Cheap

"Go and make interesting mistakes, make amazing mistakes, make glorious and fantastic mistakes. Break rules. Leave the world more interesting for your being here." - Neil Gaiman (author)

The number one spot I see bands and artists waste money is on recording. It's just too easy to record everything DIY nowadays for so cheap. I have produced albums for bands, solo artists, EDM and rap. I've mixed rap songs, acoustic, jazz, rock, reggae. I've also scored commercials and film. You can make professional recordings and if you're serious about your music career you should start investing some serious time into learning how to do this.

Here are two general rules of thumb to follow for recording:

1.   Your final recording MUST sound professionally recorded, mixed and mastered. Garage recordings are not acceptable.

2.   More money doesn't ever mean you're going to get more value. Do you own research on every person you work with, place you're going to record or anything else for that matter when it comes to recording. Somebody claiming they worked with John Mayer on his last album might mean he grabbed the drum mics and got coffee for

everybody. It doesn't mean he was the mastermind behind the album, ask questions and be specific to truly understand somebody's credentials before you pay them and decide to work with them.

Recording basics: My first suggestion is that you learn one of the recording platforms. I'm proficient in Ableton, Logic and Pro Tools. I didn't go to school for this, I worked at it continuously and it took years (I'm still definitely not a master and I'm still learning every day). The four big ones are FL Studio, Ableton, ProTools and Logic. You can get away with Garageband as well if you're a solo singer/songwriter.

The platforms all are similar to each other but different in layout and user interface. If you're just getting started making electronic music I would suggest Ableton – if you're just getting started out with recording as a solo musician or band I would suggest Logic. There are shelves of books out there about these platforms so I'm not going to go too far into depth about this, you'll need to do your own learning and research. Recording is an art and you will learn as you go and get better over the years, don't pass up the opportunity to start learning though if you are able. Imagine if every time you had a new idea for an album you could make it for free or a couple hundred dollars instead of thousands because you rely on studio time, a producer, mixing and mastering for every song.

Even if you can just get one step of this down it can save you money. Even if you learn just how to track instruments and vocals in your house you can save big money on studio time before sending to a professional to mix. YouTube stars have learned this and are capable of cranking out a full professionally mixed song along with creative new professional videos every single week! It's not just cover songs any more either, DJs are putting out a new song a month typically with remixes weekly, even new bands are putting out a song every 6 weeks. It's slowly becoming the new standard in music.

WHAT YOU NEED TO GET STARTED RECORDING ($500-$1000):

1.   Choose your recording platform (ProTools, Logic, FL Studio, Ableton) – do research!

2.   Have a fast enough computer. I prefer Mac but know plenty of musicians that work on PC successfully

3.   You need a Digital Audio Interface. This is what you plug into your computer and plug your microphone or instrument into. It is how you record basically. It should have enough ins/outs to handle as many instruments as you would like to record at once. I personally like Focusrite products, they're a solid mid-line interface with good preamps. Spending a little money here will save you big headaches in the future. Do research.

4.   You'll need a microphone for vocals (unless you're instrumental only). You'll need to do your own research on this as well but again, spending a bit now will save you

headache in the future. A cheap microphone is the fastest way to ruin a recording. Any mixer that's fought to remove the background hum from a recording will agree. Different microphones shine better on different voices. I've used online store's (I won't name them) liberal return policy to experiment on a few different microphones. One side consideration would be a good preamp as well with a microphone. A mid-line microphone and preamp combination can work wonders. The best way to describe a preamp to somebody that knows nothing about them is to think about photography - it's like taking a picture through an iPhone and then taking the picture through a $3000 DSLR camera. You capture far more details in the right areas and everything sounds better with the right one. I can't stress enough, do research on this.

5.   Studio headphones. Any decent pair will do fine for now, $40 or so can get you what you need. You just don't want to be listening to your mix through apple earbuds whenever you want to record. Although I've done this plenty of times on the road.

TIPS FOR RECORDING:

1.   When you record check to make sure you don't red-line (play too loud) no matter how hard you play or sing into the mic. If you are you'll need to turn down the gain on your digital audio interface. It's better to come in softer than too loud.

2.   Play to a metronome when recording

3.   Drums are a beast to record. Unless you're experienced with recording I would suggest using a studio to record drums. One other suggestion is v-drums and a good MIDI drum program to get drum sounds. I've produced a full rock band album using this and industry pros couldn't tell, it can definitely be done – isn't technology amazing! Two I would suggest are FXpansion BFD3 or Superior Drummer by Toontrack, both allow you to customize the kits, brushes, drum heads, mic placements and more.

4.   Know your songs before you start recording. Have every transition, beat, lyric, solo, etc. down completely before you start recording. The studio is not the time to figure this out, although recording DIY gives you much more flexibility in this since you're never on the clock or paying per hour.

5.   Experiment, experiment, experiment. Push the limits, try different mic placements on guitar amps, use effects and plug-ins. Keep learning and do what you can to push the limits. You will need to continue to research and grow but the best time is now to start with recording.

6.   Before you record anything for the first time you should google how to do it. There will be tons of great articles on how professionals do it. SoundonSound.com is a phenomenal resource full of posts on how to record and mix. Knowing exactly where to place a mic on a guitar amp or how to capture the sound of a cello is necessary before you start experimenting.

THE NEXT THINGS TO BUY (non-necessity but certainly good to have)

- Monitors. If you're going to start mixing your own music the first thing you'll need is a pair of studio monitors. More expensive monitors will not necessarily make a huge difference until you're very trained on how to mix and what to listen for. And frankly the best mixers in the world could probably create a better mix on laptop speakers than you could on their $10,000 speakers. In my opinion, starting out a decent pair will do just fine.
- A class for recording. One class with a pro could work wonders for your recording, you can find them online for very cheap or even free. There are books and local classes as well.
- Sound absorbent studio foam - putting up sound absorbers around your room will reduce reflections from the walls of a bedroom which you're singing or playing another instrument. This is also a necessity for mixing as well. Along those same lines, a microphone shield can go a long way in reducing reflections as well. It sits behind your microphone and cuts down on unwanted sound.

So all of that was how to get started with recording on your own and compared to the cost of a producer and studio time, buying these items already saved you money. Plus you now own equipment you can grow with, I definitely suggest trying to DIY your recordings as much as possible. If you're struggling big time with recording or don't think it will be a possibility for whatever reason my next suggestion is to find somebody to help. The best thing you can do is develop (or already have) a relationship with somebody that will do it for cheap, if you don't know anybody I would suggest talking to other bands around town to see who they worked with. Find bands local to you that you like and admire and reach out to them, most will be happy to talk to you and ask them who they worked with to produce their last album. They will likely be more than happy to pass along their information and also let you know what they thought of them. You definitely want to work with one person that knows the recording process from front to back though if you have nobody in your band that does, don't just go to a studio on your own and book time. That person will likely have a relationship with a local studio to get cheaper rates and also can work on mixing and mastering for the album as well. If you're a solo musician this person will likely *be* the studio, they'll have the equipment you need to record.

If that doesn't work you could hit up Craigslist to both search for people that have already posted and make a post yourself. I would suggest posting under gigs-offered and musicians. You should at the very least have something to show them so they know your sound, if you don't have previous music an iPhone recording would do just fine for them. They just want to hear what your sound is to see if they want to work with you. You can be honest in the post as well, you'll save yourself and the potential producers a lot of time by letting them know you're on a fairly tight budget to see if they could work with you. Everything is a negotiation! Here's an example of an ad I would post on Craiglist to find a good producer:

Post Title – Blues-Rock Band Looking For Producer

Local blues-rock band looking for assistance recording and producing upcoming EP. Our songs are written and ready to go now we need to get them recorded. We're looking to work with somebody that can help us do this. We have four instruments: guitar, bass, drums and keys. We understand we'll have to pay but also we're a band lol…so our budget is a bit tight, would love to develop a relationship for more recording and sounds as well in the future. You can check out low quality recordings here of the songs we want to record (SOUNDCLOUD LINK).

If you like the music and want to work together let us know and reply via text XXX-XXX-XXXX.

Thanks,

Brad

Tweak the message to fit your style as needed. The next thing you'll want to do is to check out what they've done. Unless somebody is willing to work for free, do not work with anybody without vetting them. First you'll want to listen to songs they've done and ask specifically what role they played in the recordings. Did they do everything? Just mixing? Were they an audio engineer? The role they played in those songs matters a lot. Listen to the quality in the recordings and look for artists similar to yourself.

Once you have your short-list of producers you can meet with them to see if you get along with them and can work with them easily. Discuss the price in detail. It's not uncommon to pay per hour for a producer's time, ask how you will be able to track how many hours they are spending. Will there be caps on this rate or can they just charge whatever time they want per song? Would they be willing to work for a flat rate per song or for the entire album? Do they want a percentage of royalties on the album instead of cash up front. Many will be open to ideas and if they believe in your music could be open to a percentage of royalties. This makes your relationship more like a partnership and perhaps would be better for an on-going relationship in the future as well.

Whatever you agree upon be thorough, direct and honest about what you would like and what you want to spend. It will save you time and arguments down the road. If you find somebody that can get your songs professionally recorded for cheap, keep them – they are a huge asset.

If you can't find anybody to record you and you can't do it yourself you're not completely out of luck. You can call local recording studios (quick Google search will turn some up) and give them the same pitch as the Craigslist post. They'll be happy to work with you as well and usually offer mixing, mastering, recording, etc. packages that are all inclusive. This is similar to taking care of your car – you can learn to work on it yourself, you can find a good mechanic or the most expensive option would be taking it to the dealer. You know the dealer (the studio) will give you great work but you'll be paying top price usually for this work.

I recently saw two local indie artists produce albums, one spent $30,000 and the other spend $40,000. Neither of them had budgets left-over afterwards for marketing and the albums basically did nothing. My band's latest 10 track album cost us $1000 total to produce, we negotiated $100 per song from a top mixer and relationship we developed over a few years and recorded everything on our own for free. Their albums were great but so was ours...even professional ears wouldn't know the differences (one single from the album was selected by iHeart Radio in 2016 for their rising star search and made it into the top 10). It's 2017, learn how to do this stuff on your own.

One other notable resource I just began using is called soundbetter.com. This is like a virtual marketplace for top level mixers, producers, vocalists and musicians for hire. I successfully hired somebody to do mixing/mastering on my last album from soundbetter from Austin that I probably never would have found on my own. You can create a post for free and submit to professionals and get quotes from them. Follow all the same guidelines I mentioned before when vetting these professionals.

Chapter 4 – A Website, Socials and Email - Working Together For You

"Social Media is about the people! Not about your business. Provide for the people and the people will provide for you." - Matt Goulart (founder of Ignite Digital Inc.)

The world we live in is a digital age, social media matters. I know it sucks doesn't it? Nobody likes to stop whatever they're doing to live-stream a video to Facebook or Twitter and say what's up to fans, but I guarantee you'll be happy when 200 more fans come to your show the next night...can you say #BLESSED?

I'm going to get into each platform individually later on, how to set them up, use them effectively and how to develop your marketing campaigns on each one. For this chapter I'm just going to talk basics and a little marketing theory as well.

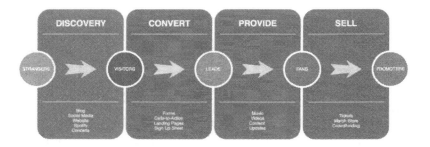

Remember when I said your music isn't your product, it's just marketing content? Well so are all your social media profiles and your website. Your website, Twitter, Facebook, Instagram, YouTube, SnapChat, ReverbNation, SoundCloud, Vimeo, Pandora, Spotify and everywhere else your music, videos and pictures are should act like fingers on the end of a hand on the end of an arm all designed like a big funnel to find more people and bring them into your brand. The goal when somebody goes through your funnel will change - for applications it's to get a download, for a website it might be to get somebody to purchase or create an account. Your goal at the end of this funnel is typically going to be getting an email address (or other opt-in) from somebody that previously was not a fan of your music so you can develop your relationship with them and eventually sell to them in the future.

Email open rates for musicians sit around 22% - a well opted in email list could be higher as well, my general fan list is around a 36% open rate and targeted city based campaigns can be as high as 60% or more. Follow up emails after shows are around 80 or 90%. Sorry, I told you I would keep stats out of this and just tell you what to do.

Just trust me on this, it's way higher than your social media posts are getting. An email is a phenomenal form of "opting-in". Another reason you want to get an email address over just a page like is that social media platforms are changing constantly. Facebook constantly changes their policies for band and musician pages. Everybody that built up millions of Vine followers pretty much lost out when Vine went under. Myspace, well you know what happened there. Your social media fans are not fans you own...the platform actually owns and controls your relationship with your followers. Once you have an email you have a way of making contact when you need to for free (or very cheap). One step further would be to get a phone number from fans so you could text them about upcoming shows when you're in town.

To quickly wrap up this chapter, when you think of social media as the fingers of the funnel to get people to opt in to your email list it becomes a little less pointless and a little more of a smart way to grow your fan base and connect with them. Remember that concept when you interact on each platform, use each one properly, don't tie them all together with auto-posts even though it saves time (except for show dates from SongKick or Reverbnation) and use it to actually connect with people that like your music.

Respond to your messages, reply to comments that deserve comments, retweet interesting things you think your fans would like, re-gram and live stream videos of practice, tour bus life, hanging out, etc. Be accessible, that's what the music industry is now...artists are accessible to their fans and you should be too if you want to keep them. Typically the artists that are the best at this are naturally younger because they've grown up with it. If you struggle with this I would suggest finding a few popular younger artists and following all their social media platforms to see what they do. Remember their target audience might be different than yours, if you're a classic rock band you don't need to make cute bubbly videos aimed at 15 year olds but you can definitely pick up tips and tricks on what they're doing in each post, video and picture they create.

Chapter 5 - Your Email List

"If you're not building an email list, you're an idiot. I know that's harsh, but when a company can destroy your entire business with one fell swoop, you should rely on things you can control." - Derek Halpern (founder of Social Triggers, Inc.)

We'll start with the email list since I said it's the foundation of contacting your fans and your funnel. You need a flexible well regarded email client that doesn't get flagged as spam when you send to users and also one that allows you to be a little flexible with how your add members to your list. You don't want to get somebody's email from them in person while you're having lunch and go to add them to your list and they have to confirm the opt-in again to actually receive emails from you. Also, you don't want a flexible grey hat service that gets your email moved to junk by big email clients like Gmail and Yahoo mail.

My suggestion for this is to set up an account with MailChimp, it's free **with limited features** up to a certain number of email addresses. If you're completely against MailChimp for whatever reason I could also suggest Constant Contact, I used to use them a bunch and know they're capable of all the same things as MailChimp. These are cheap enough and will give you everything you need to be successful.

To really take advantage and use the email list to its fullest extent you should sign up for the next level MailChimp package, they call it "growing business", and it will be about $15-20 per month to start.

To successfully use your email list you need to know a bit about email marketing terms and theory first though.

When somebody signs up for your email newsletter they will be added to a **list**. You can have multiple lists and you can control which sign-ups go to which lists. For example if somebody exchanges an email for a free album download on your website they can go to your "website signup" list. This will help you follow up appropriately and also can help to measure what marketing campaigns are working best.

When you create an email you can save that email as a custom **template**. So if you brand with your logos and colors you can quickly pull that up again and just add content. I suggest saving a template for new song, new video, new shows, and general emails.

Once somebody signs up you can create an **automated email campaign** that they'll get without you doing anything. That means in the example of a website sign-up that they would automatically receive an email after they sign up with a free download to your album. Without you doing anything you can create an email that follows up seven days later with a personalized message asking them if they liked it and a link to your latest video. Then ten days after that you could send them a link to your new album and three days after that a direct link to buy merch or sign up for your Patreon account.

Spam is when you email people promotionally without their permission to do so. The reason you can't just email 200,000 random email addresses is because you will be spamming them and your email client will shut you down. If your email client doesn't shut you down, Gmail (and other email clients) will identify you as spam and may also identify your website as a spam website (if you use a booking@bandname.com email) to reach out. They'll also identify links in the email as spam. If you abuse this is could have major effects on your ability to operate in the future and your website's SEO ranking.

A **sign-up page** is a landing page designed with one purpose, to get people to sign-up for your email list. You can have 40 different sign-up pages for different things and testing, testing and more testing is the best way to figure out what page converts a person from checking out your music to signed up on your list. Sign-up pages can be easily created through a lot of different tools, MailChimp offers a free simple sign-up page creator that will be automatically linked to a corresponding email list.

The show sign-up: I suggest at the minimum getting an email and a first name from everybody that signs up. The first name will allow you to personalize your emails which means it's more likely to get opened, not get flagged as spam and it feels a bit more personalized for your fans. You should also create **sub-lists** inside your lists when somebody signs up from a show, if you filter by "date added" you can name each show date and city in your sub-list. This will help you to target that same list when you go back to town. Organizing your lists is crucial for marketing correctly to them, you never want to hit up somebody in LA to let them know you're playing in San Francisco (I've done it) but on the other hand a personalized message goes a very long way. If your list is already created and you don't have city information MailChimp now offers location services which segments the list by location based on open data from other clients and IP addresses, I've found it to be very accurate as well but would still suggest segmenting just to be sure.

Here's an example email to send, you can add the metadata tag {first name} to the start of the email to automatically populate the first name of your fan.

Hey Julie,

It was great meeting you last time we were in town at House of Blues. Just want to let you know we'll be back your way this Friday playing a show at Belly Up Tavern with some rad local bands. Would love to see you out, tickets are $10 at the door and *if you bring a friend your first drinks on us. Let us know if you're coming out, email or text at XXX-XXX-XXXX with any questions or to let us know, much love!*

Brad

Notice a few things from that email. Nothing was in third person, everything was "you" and "us" in the email to feel more personalized and connected. For that email I wouldn't put it on a formal header with pictures either, that's just a straight-forward email you send that let's somebody know you're coming to town and that you would love to see them out. It feels like you are just emailing her about it. The same way I'm writing this book just to you.

You can have less personalized emails too, when you release a new song you don't need to always make it seem like you're writing just the person directly. It's okay to just announce new music, you should always encourage an action though in every email. It should only be one action per email....I repeat, ONLY ONE ACTION PER EMAIL. Don't say, "we just put out our newest music video, check it out here and also we launched our Kickstarter campaign for our next album. You can donate here. Finally we're going tour this summer, click here for all the show dates." You'll confuse people, most people only have time to do one thing so focus on that whatever it is.

MailChimp has a free app called MailChimp Subscribe for tablets you can use to get sign-ups at your show. **If I can make one huge suggestion it would be that you take this seriously.** If you have an iPad you can use that, if you don't have a tablet you can buy a $40-$80 Google tablet and set it up just for this purpose at shows. It's a signup list you can customize so people can enter their email address and signup for your list. This saves you time on transferring emails after each show from a list that are typically written down by drunk people in chicken scratches and allows you to give people instant gratification. The setup I use says in big letters at the top of the screen, "SIGN UP BELOW FOR A FREE DOWNLOAD OF MY ALBUM". Below that there is a box to type their name and email (and phone number if you want that) with a button that says "SEND ME THE ALBUM". From there they instantly receive an email, usually they receive it right in front of me on their phones while we're still talking. Ten days later they get my video and a few days after I ask them to like my Facebook page, etc.

Another great feature for clubs and also festival shows, if you don't have a wifi connection it will save the email addresses until you have connectivity and then will add them all to the list. While you're playing you should have somebody walking around that is outgoing and personable getting people to sign up for the list. After somebody signs up for this, the show sign-up list open rate sits in the 80% range for me. If you don't have anybody to walk around for you I suggest after you play to walk around yourself, introduce yourself and offer a free download of your album if they sign up. I got 80 sign-ups in 15 minutes the first time I tried this just by walking around to tables in between sets at a hotel. That's a gig I usually wrote off as just a paycheck but suddenly it turned it into a fantastic way to accumulate more fans. Plus walking around yourself is a great way to make a new deeper connection with people that have been listening to you.

Beyond your fans you'll want to create separate lists for press, industry contacts, bookers and festivals. I'll discuss outreach to them in future chapters, you'll definitely want them organized in separate lists from what you send to your fans though so you can easily reach out to them when you have a new tour announcement, press release, music release or anything else you may want to just communicate to them.

The more work you put into organizing your email list early on, creating email templates, automated email chains, etc. the more effective you will be in the long run and the less work you'll have to do to reach out to your fans when you need to. I'll get into all the other apps to use with your email client in further chapters.

Chapter 6 – Building Your Website and EPK

"Any idiot can put up a website" - Patricia Briggs

If you don't have a website I suggest you try to build this on your own. Here's why, first it's just way too easy nowadays to do this through WordPress or Squarespace and second, when you need something updated you won't have to call a friend/family member or worse, a web developer that will charge you. Your website is a tool for you as an artist, what the site looks like, feels like, how it operates and what it does for you is completely up to you. Sometimes you might want the site to just be one music video with a "subscribe" button next to it. Other times it might be where you lead people to sell tickets for the upcoming tour. The site can be fluid, you can change it when you want to and you can track how people interact with your website.

I like Squarespace if you have never set up a website before, it's very user friendly and can create beautiful websites quickly. One other website creation tool I recently got turned onto was PageCloud, it is very simple to use for anybody to create a great website with everything you would need.

You should have two different websites or web-addresses you can lead people to. They will function very differently but they will both be yours. One will be for fans to go to and that is your regular website. The other will be for anybody in the industry (press, bookers, PR, agents, labels, etc.) to go to learn more about you. This is called your EPK. Do not try to mix the two together into one site, it's a fast way to have a bad website for fans that also is tough for industry contacts to navigate. My suggestion is that you have a link on the regular site for "press" that leads to the other website. That website can be a reflection of your current site - www.bandname.com/epk - for example.

Your website is a direct reflection of your brand so it should have a look and feel that's identifiable to you. There's no right way to set up your website, if you look at 20 popular musicians they'll all have different websites with completely different looks. The best thing you can do is ask yourself what you want the website to do for you and why you're building it or changing it when you do this. Don't overwhelm a fan that is going to be looking at you for the first time but give them a way to find what they would want. It's okay to have different versions of your website or landing pages for people to hit depending on where they're coming from. If they signed up at a show and are visiting for the first time from the email they received maybe you want them to land on something that thanks them for taking the time and rewards them. If they're coming to your site from a particular music video you just released maybe you would have a behind the scenes video first to give them extra information about that video. Not everybody that goes to your site is looking for the same thing and people nowadays do not have time to spend clicking around and searching for what they wanted, give them the experience they want right off the bat and make it as simple to access as possible. The only way you can do all this testing and creation is if you control and make the site yourself though.

Here are some website no-nos to follow when creating the site:

- Don't make a website so crazy it takes forever to load.
- Don't host music on your own website using the site's music tool, you should embed music from SoundCloud or Spotify to get the plays and also because their platform will be more stable.
- Don't have a video or audio that auto-plays with sound when somebody opens the page. That's annoying to everybody, if somebody wants to play your video they'll click the giant play button over it
- Don't forget about "contact us" – let people know how to get a hold of you
- Don't host videos on your website, embed from Vimeo or YouTube
- Don't forget to include links to your socials
- Don't forget to have an email signup spot – this could be in exchange for songs or whatever attractive offer you want to give. Make sure people can find it really easy.

I personally think a website can be a hub of your socials. It's easy to have an automatically updated feed from Instagram for your pictures section. You can embed your YouTube videos easily on there. If you want you can even add a Facebook and Twitter feed. If you're playing shows I suggest adding your shows to the website by embedding a Songkick widget. If you're not on Songkick you should go sign up immediately and add your show dates. It's an app that allows you to update all your shows as they come up, you can install it on your Facebook page as well, it integrates with Spotify and most local papers and blogs automatically pull shows from Songkick to list in their "what's happening" page. I suggest also having a press area on your website that is constantly updated with the latest press you get.

Again, I've seen some big artists that have website with just a music video and an email sign-up form underneath along the video with a link to the store. I've also seen sites with everything I mentioned as well as a full blog. When you consider the design of your site I suggest you think about your fans first so you design around what they would appreciate from you. Next you think about the purpose of the site and what you want it to do. Do you want to sell merch? Do you want to keep a blog that people would be interested in reading weekly? Do you want to make a big hub of all your information? Do you just want to show people your latest music video? Design around these basic ideas and you won't fail.

The final piece is that you have to be able to track what people do on your website. It's a major piece of everything you do from a marketing perspective. If you go on tour for example and have 20 cities you're selling tickets in and run a $2000 ad campaign and sell $3,000 worth of tickets you need to know if they all came from that campaign first of all. Next you need to be able to consider adjustments to sell more tickets, maybe the $2,000 advertisement actually had 8 different forms of the same ad and only 1 of them actually sold tickets while 7 wasted money. Before putting in more money you need to be able to track which ones worked best and only use that. It's simple stuff once all this is in place but it starts with being able to track conversions on your site. Google Analytics is free and is a very robust tool that generates statistics about visitors to your website. Where they're coming from, how often they come back, and what they're doing while they're there. Once you understand and are using Google Analytics fully you'll be ready for more sophisticated tools, there are a number of click tracking tools out there and each offer different benefits depending on your needs. If you're at that point it's very likely you'll know what you're looking for.

Applications to use on your website (this list will assuredly change so do research):

- Soundcloud.com – the easiest way to allow people to stream your music directly from your site
- YouTube.com – the easiest way to embed videos on your website
- Toneden.io – Advanced social and email sign-up gate application. Toneden has some of the best

tools for engaging new fans. There is a full suite of tools for music marketing. One of the best I've seen includes a "Social media like to download gate that automatically pulls email information, location and social interests. You should definitely sign up and experiment with their tools.

- Limitedrun.com – Band merchandise direct to fans with easy to use templates and a flat fee rather than percentage of sales

Next up is your EPK. An EPK is your Electronic Press Kit, anybody you approach in the music industry should get a link to your EPK. Your EPK is a separate site from your website and is geared towards industry insiders. Bloggers, critics, labels, bookers, agents and managers will all want to look at your EPK. Again, there is no correct format for an EPK but I can tell you a few things that you definitely don't want to do to start:

- Don't have your EPK on the same web page as your regular fan site (or at least have a link on your fan website to a separate page for your EPK)
- Don't leave any information out of your EPK. Include everything that's relevant
- Don't make it tough to find information on the EPK site, it should be simple and organized
- It doesn't have to be pretty. Music industry contacts don't need all the fluff which makes a slower experience for them. They're trying to do work and want to get to the information they need as fast as possible.

Just like your website, you should think about the purpose of your EPK. When you contact a local paper to write about you they will want to be able to find all the information they need as quickly as possible to write an interesting article about you. If they have to dig for information they'll pass you up. I know this for a fact because I ran a music review blog so I learned what it's like to be approached by musicians that want you to write about them. Before I even listened to their music I checked them out to see if I could quickly gather enough information to write an article. If they didn't have their shit together I passed, I didn't even listen to their music. I just had too many other bands that made my job simpler so I could listen to their music and write a review without having to dig through google to put together an article.

This goes for bookers as well. If a venue booker can't quickly find your past shows and live videos immediately they'll take a pass before going any further. Has a band ever approached you to play a show and left you struggling to figure out what their sound is like while you click through their site and search on YouTube or other social networks to figure it out. You probably don't deal with hundreds of bands contacting you about bookings so you may have spent the time looking it up. A booker will not spend that time, make it simple for them.

Just like your website, think about what you're going after with your EPK during different points of your career and manage the site appropriately. Are you looking for management, bookings, press, tour support, labels, investor funding? Create your EPK as such and edit as needed. Here are some things you'll definitely need on there:

- Live Videos and music videos – both streaming embedded and download links in case a news channel or other media spot wants to air your video and needs an MP4 version
- All your music, streaming and download links
- In depth artist bio including history
- Quotes page – this can be quotes from lyrics or direct quotes that press could use in their articles
- Press Release Section – all your press releases should be organized and your most current one should be at the forefront
- Past Shows – I like to include show posters with this as well
- Social media links and fan numbers easily accessible
- Anything else that makes you special and unique should be featured

Both your website and your EPK are very important pieces of your brand. Always think of what the point of each site is and update them as needed. Are you releasing a new album? That might be a good time to promote only that on your website, many bands will do a countdown timer on their site until the new album is launched. Are you going on a nationwide tour, you could make your landing page a list of dates with an email sign-up for fans next to each city for

30% off tickets. Just like your email list and your social media accounts (coming up next) your website is not something that's just there because you need it to look professional, it's a tool that can grow your fans and sell your products.

Chapter 7 - Social Media Basics

"The more social media we have, the more we think we're connecting, yet we are really disconnecting from each other." - JR (French photographer and artist)

If your brand is a giant music making, show playing, merch selling giant then social media is the arms of the giant that reach out to pull people in, shake their hands and hold them close. Use each platform how it is supposed to be used and those arms will get more people to listen to your music and connect with your brand – if you master it and give them great content and experiences you'll keep them for life. On the other end of the spectrum, if you don't know what you're doing you can spend a ton of money on ad revenue and get very little or nothing out of it. It's pretty amazing how fast $100 can go on Facebook ads, if you've run a Facebook ad campaign before you know what I'm talking about – and if you do it wrong you'll form no connection with those fans you reach out to and the money will be wasted.

Remember that social media is a way to connect with people on a massive scale but never forget about the word *connection* - root it deeply in everything you do. Picture every social interaction as a real life conversation. If somebody walked up to you after a show and said, "hi, I love your music" you would say thanks and talk with them a bit, ask them where they heard it and get to know them.

What if you didn't respond to them or just simply said thanks? They would feel unappreciated and maybe would think differently of you.

Everybody that follows you on these platforms wants to get a glimpse of your life. The majority of them are working shit jobs, they're stuck in class, they're driving through traffic - the list goes on - they want to see what your rock star life is like. They don't want to hear about how hard it is to sell a record or how shitty the fans were last night. Whatever you do, don't ever post that kind of negative content. They want to be amazed just like they would be if they came to a show. This is another outlet for you to be creative: make fun games for fans, let them join in contests, ask them questions, let them pick your next cover, etc. Stick to what your brand is and don't try to be something you're not just because it works for another artist.

Each platform is a bit different in rules, best practices, etc. so I'll go through them individually for you and how to effectively market and build a fan base on each.

Chapter 8 - Twitter

"The best way to engage honestly with the marketplace via Twitter is to never use the words 'engage', 'honesty', or 'marketplace'." - Jeffrey Zeldman

I have found Twitter to be my least favorite platform to update or use in my personal life but the best site for finding new fans of my brand. I just felt it was a less personal version of Facebook until I really started diving deeper into all the capabilities of the site. Once you really get into it, Twitter can be the most powerful tool you have to find new fans and connect with them.

I'm not going to tell you exactly what to post, that's highly personal to your brand – keep it consistent as always with who you are and what your fans expect. As a general rule of thumb, photos and videos are far more engaging than simple text. Also, because of the way Twitter is set up, it's common to tweet the same thing a few times in a day as well since people may miss it in their feed, it's not like Facebook if you're used to that. Just keep your page interesting always, try to use a profile picture of your face (or faces for a band) and not a symbol or picture. You'll get far better engagement with an actual profile picture of you, also make sure you keep the link and short bio updated so people can quickly see who you are when they connect. These are the first things people look at when they find you so you want this to be a reflection of your brand in a few short words and a **call-to-action** they can take like downloading your music, signing up for your fan club, buying merch, etc.

There is a formula for marketing on Twitter to find new fans, it's pretty simple. First, I recommend you get a Twitter plugin like Tweepi or Crowdfire (which can also work with Instagram). These are powerful apps that allow you to perform highly target searches through Twitter to find new people that would be likely to enjoy your music and follow those people in masses. Beyond that you can also sort through the fans that didn't follow you back and unfollow them to make sure you don't follow too many people, the ratio of followers vs. how many you're following matters both when people look at your page and also to Twitter because they impose limits on those ratios and will not allow you to follow more people until you get more followers. When you connect Tweepi to your Twitter account you'll be able to search for all sorts of people. I recommend starting by searching for followers of a user that is similar to you, in the same locations you're targeting, genre, etc. Once you do that put them into an app like Tweepi and you're going to see a list of all their current followers, these are people that are opted into that artist and currently follow them. The next step will be to filter through those users to get down to the individuals that you want to target, here is an example of an exact filter sequence I've used to find followers.

- Followers of: @officialkaleo
- Last Tweeted Date | is newer than | 20 days ago

- Follow Ratio | is less than | 100 - *(Meaning they follow back when you follow them)*
- Language | is | English (or whatever language you want)
- Last action (via Tweepi) | is empty

This means that I'm going to only see users that follow @officialkaleo that have tweeted sometime in the last 20 days so I knew they're active, with a high follow-back ratio, that speaks English and that I haven't previously followed via tweepi. This is a subset that I can work with and begin to follow without wasting my time on people that are unlikely to enjoy my music.

Once you generate that list you can begin following those users. If you're using Tweepi, I'd recommend downloading a Tweepi plugin for Chrome that will allow you to mass follow all of them in the list so you don't have to click on each follow button one at a time.

You can follow up to 950 users per day, not all of them will follow you back but if you're set up right a good percentage of them will follow you back. From there you can set up an auto-message through Crowdfire that will message them directly once they follow you. Here a quick example of an intro message I use to automatically message new people that follow me:

thanks for the follow, hit us up whenever...let us know what you think of our new songs or any covers you'd like to hear. If you haven't listened to us yet, check us out...we're a mix of blues-rock, soul and a touch of reggae. When you have a minute, check out this music video of ours and let us know if you dig it! (link) ... - we'll send you some free tunes if you want, just let us know.

Stay engaged with these messages because they will definitely write you back and want to talk to you, don't deny them this – be real and authentic and form a connection just like you're talking in person. If they like it you can give them a link to download your latest album for free - this will take them to an email signup page and once they enter their email they'll automatically get the download sent to them, now you have their email.

I suggest keeping it fairly informal with this intro message as well. Notice my grammar isn't perfect, it's written using the words "I", "you" and "we" and it feels a bit like a real message I sent. Most that are familiar with Twitter will know this is an automated direct message but will still engage nonetheless, check out your music and stay in touch. In fairness I've also read marketing suggestions for Twitter that recommend not using an auto-DM to message people because so many use it and it feels unauthentic. I personally like it because it works but I just wanted to acknowledge that some people will tell you not to. Again, it's up to you...if you think it keeps up with your brand and will work I say you should test it, it's a great tool to form connections.

The next piece of the puzzle is the Unfollow. You'll want to use Tweepi to filter out people that don't follow up back because Twitter has ratios and numbers that enforce your follower vs. followed-by percentage. As a rule of thumb you don't want to be following more people than are following you – it's dumb, I know, but this is what you need to do. Filter a search for people that you followed more than 14 days ago that do not follow you back and unfollow them, you can use the chrome plugin to quickly automate this process as well. This will keep your page fresh and keep your fan base growing every single day.

Once you get this process down you should be able to do this in about 5 minutes or less every day - for a little money per month you can upgrade and automate this process, I think it's worth it to automate the process once you understand how to do it so it runs on autopilot for you. Don't miss a day, this is a very fast way to grow and engage new fans online so you can continue to create a foster a connection. Post your new videos on your page, music, sign-up links, free downloads, show dates, etc. Twitter is a tool you can't ignore and if used correctly can grow your fan base very quickly and targeted. As with everything in this book, do research and consider other options besides the tools I gave you – new sites pop up every 5 minutes so the next great marketing app for Twitter might not even be invented as I write this.

Chapter 9 - Instagram

"Instagram. Pictures. Lots of pictures! I don't really care to read everyone's thoughts." - Christina Milian

Instagram started out as a photo-sharing and simple photo-editing app. It still is that but also now allows video clips as well as live video streaming and "stories" which was launched in direct competition to Snapchat's stories. Instagram was bought by Facebook in 2012 and now allows direct advertisements inside the platform which can be integrated into your Facebook campaign as well with a one-click integration from your Facebook ads account page.

I almost don't want to repeat this but some of you assuredly skipped other parts of the book so I have to. **When you consider what you're posting on Instagram you need to think mainly about your brand, who you are and what your fans want.** If you're a Christian Rock band you shouldn't post pictures of you back stage getting wasted. Nobody cares to see pictures that don't pertain to you or your brand on your Instagram so no pictures of just your friends, inside jokes that only the band gets or basically anything else that doesn't apply to you. The most important thing is to KEEP YOUR PAGE INTERESTING so people want to follow you and see what you're all about. Your profile picture should be one of you, not a symbol or picture of your album. Finally you should use your description wisely, make a direct call-to-action that people can click to download your latest tune, sign up for your email list or check out your latest video. Whatever you are pushing should be reflected right at the top of your profile. Whatever pictures, video clips you share, make sure to post regularly – on Instagram that means once every day or two. As much as possible (like 90% of the time or more) you should try to put yourself into the pictures; you're not a company, you are a musician so let people see you and what your life is all about, that's what people want access to.

Marketing on Instagram works similar to Twitter. There are a lot of apps out there to assist with this but Crowdfire, FollowMe, Instagress and Followers all work well I've found with different features and benefits. I like Crowdfire since it is already working for my Twitter account, you might as well keep it all in the same place and just have one link to bookmark when you're running your social media marketing. Just like Twitter you can run search campaigns to hone in on specific Instagram users and filter based on criteria like who they follow, hashtags they've used, searches and more. You can mass follow groups that will likely also be into your page and then set up unfollow campaigns for users that haven't followed you back after a certain amount of time. I'm not going to go deep into this again because I just talked all about following campaigns in the previous chapter.

I caution you, as Instagram/Twitter as well as these apps change policies often, you may need to do a little research before just haphazardly following thousands of people in a day. As I write this the landscape is changing for marketing tools as well, what worked today might not work tomorrow. Spend some time researching first. Start out slow if you've never done this before and remember it's a long marathon, not a sprint. You won't build up a 100k following in a week, nor should you try. Shoot for about 100 new followers a week to start and let that naturally grow as you continue to post great content and keep up a strong outreach. Always make sure to recognize the difference between a follower and an engaged follower. If you're building up by 1000 people a week but none of them are liking or commenting on your posts you're doing something wrong, try to critically think about what's going on and adjust your content or your outreach to retarget and refocus your efforts.

Chapter 10 - YouTube

"I just made my album. I did my best. And I uploaded the video just to 'YouTube.' That was all." - Psy

YouTube has made music sharing and discovery easier than it's ever been in history. Here are some fun facts for you according to YouTube (2017):

Global Reach:

- YouTube has over a billion users — almost one-third of all people on the Internet — and every single day people watch hundreds of millions of hours on YouTube and generate billions of views.
- YouTube overall, and even YouTube on mobile alone, reaches more 18-34 and 18-49 year-olds than any cable network in the U.S.
- More than half of YouTube views come from mobile devices.
- YouTube has launched local versions in more than 88 countries.
- You can navigate YouTube in a total of 76 different languages (covering 95% of the Internet population).

Investing in Creators:

- The number of channels earning six figures per year on YouTube is up 50% y/y.   The YouTube Spaces team is focused on helping creators make great content through strategic programs and workshops largely administered at the YouTube Space production facilities in Los Angeles, New York, London, Tokyo, Sao Paulo and Berlin.
- As of March 2015, creators filming in YouTube Spaces have produced over 10,000 videos which have generated over 1 billion views and 70+ million hours of watch time.

Copyright:

- As of July 2016, YouTube has paid out $2 billion to rights holders who have chosen to monetize claims since Content ID first launched in 2007.
- As of July 2015, there are 8,000+ partners using Content ID — including many major network broadcasters, movie studios and record labels — who have claimed over 400 million videos, helping them control their content on YouTube and make money on videos containing copyrighted material.
- We have more than 50 million active reference files in our Content ID database, making it the most comprehensive in the world. It's even won a PrimeTime Emmy!

Video is here to stay and if video is not a major piece of your strategy right now you need to change that. Video is the common theme exploding as well on Facebook, Instagram, Twitter, SnapChat and pretty much everywhere else on the web. In the same way the birth of MTV made the music video important, YouTube is making video beyond the music video important. It's become so easy to capture high quality video, edit the video and share with the world that it's becoming expected nowadays that you do it.

An important thing to consider when creating the video content you'll put on YouTube is to consider your audience. If you're going after the millennial audience you should research the channels that are out there right now doing this. YouTube Creators in the music space are unique, the most famous channels have created ways to continue to create very high quality audio and video productions on a weekly basis. Repetition is a major theme in these channels; just like your favorite TV show, you want to be able to tune in at a certain time of the week and see what's next. YouTube takes this to the next level though through all its social functionality.

It's easy to forget sometimes that YouTube is a social network, just like Facebook and Twitter. Many musicians fall into the trap of thinking it's just a place to post a video and that's it. The comments, follows, likes, shares and direct messages are all self-contained within the network itself, you have to treat YouTube as a community. It's amazing what a simple reply can do for a super fan that just said they loved your video – in the same regard if you ignore your YouTube videos and treat the site simply as a hosting network for your videos and that's it you can lose fans that perhaps wanted to interact with you.

The best way to use YouTube is to maximize the tools and features to build up a following continuously while interacting with the community of YouTube. By doing this you'll reach more people and over the course of time you'll ultimately move them towards your email gate where you'll capture their email and add them to your list for future direct marketing and outreach.

First you'll need to set up your channel. You can choose a profile picture (I always recommend one with your face) and also a banner for your channel. Follow the YouTube guidelines to create your banner, if there is anything unique about your YouTube channel you can include it there like "subscribe for a new cover song every Tuesday at 7pm". Next of course you'll need videos. If you just have one video than set up your channel with that one video but put it into a playlist as well on the channel, maybe it's "cover songs" or "originals", etc. This will allow you to continue to build off that and create your playlist so people can continuously stream your music when they hit your channel. A playlist is a simple way to keep people moving through your videos after they've finished one, otherwise YouTube might suggest they listen to another band next that's similar to you and then you'll lose a potential subscriber.

What if you don't have video? Frankly, every song you put out nowadays should have a video. I repeat, every song you put out on all social networks should have a video.

The simplest way to do this would be to simply play the song with a static image of your album title or artwork. To get a little more creative you can create a lyrics video easily with something like Final Cut or Adobe Premier (both are video editing software). Even simple songs with lyrics bouncing on the screen get far more plays and listens than audio alone, it gives fans something to look at while they're listening and gives your music a better chance of being listened to while people scroll through their daily feed.

The next level up would be to film a low budget music video. One way you can do this is to put an ad up on Craigslist or social media that you're looking for a talented film student to help with a music video, film students will work on projects like this for little to no pay as they build their resume. If you're working with a film student you will also typically get the benefit of working with somebody that's younger and probably keeps track of popular music video trends. Where they shine in cost they will likely lack in professionalism so you typically will need to keep that in mind. Doing your homework before shooting will pay off huge in the long run. Make sure all your shots are planned in advance, location scout before shooting, ensure your actors (if you have actors) understand the full concept of the video and give them all their call-times and make sure to define who will be the director for this video. Will you call the shots while the film student captures them or is he/she going to be making all the decisions for the shoot? Working this out beforehand will save you from showing up on the day-of and wasting everybody's time.

When scoping out whether you'll work with somebody ask to see their previous work and clarify which piece of the video they handled. Were they just a cameraman or did they direct the entire video? Did they use their own cameras or would you need to rent a camera to get this level of quality? What about lighting? Would they be doing the editing or do you need to hire a video editor after the shoot to put the video together? Be as thorough as possible when interviewing who you will be working with.

Some tips for creating music videos: if you're going to be singing along to the song make sure you have a loud system that allows you to hear the music over everything else that might be going on around you. If you're off just a bit from singing with the song it becomes very noticeable. Don't take the first price quote you get, shop around. Try to find somebody that is passionate about your music and this project. The clearer your vision is before filming, the better the video will come together in the end.

Once you've created your video or videos you can upload them to YouTube. I will get into Facebook in a moment but you cannot just upload your video to YouTube anymore, you must also upload your video to Facebook as they have a completely different video platform and network. Once you have at least one video up on a channel you can begin your marketing efforts on YouTube.

I have spent a great deal of time and money trying different things to get more views or likes on YouTube. There are a lot of services out there offering this so be very careful – some offer a specific amount of views, likes and subscribers for a set price. These are not real viewers that are listening to your music or potential fans of your band that they will get, these are machine IP addresses that will fool YouTube's video system into thinking more people have watched your video. They will get your numbers up but most of you have no reason to do this outside of your own ego. I recommend against all of these services (including Facebook likes, follows, etc.) as anybody in the industry can quickly spot a fake. YouTube has its own advertising service through Adwords that you can use as well to get more views. These will be real people but since they are advertisements your actual engagement levels are typically going to be low. Have you seen the videos that play at the beginning of a video you actually want to watch, you have to wait 5 seconds until you can skip them and that's what most people will do. You'll get the "view" counted on your video but did you really just get an engaged fan?

I've found two platforms I've used (I'm sure there are more) that really do work on YouTube though. The two I've used are TubeAssist and TubePromoter. These platforms allow you to personally reach mass amounts of users through messages, comments and subscribing to channels on automated systems.

You can set up a campaign on YouTube to target users that have interacted with videos similar to yours based on search terms you set. From there you can set up a message or multiple messages to be sent out to those users with a link to your video. This is a numbers game but if you create a well formed message you'll convert high numbers of people to go watch your video and interact with your channel. You can also comment on similar videos and subscribe to channels of users that have comments or interactions with similar videos. The software programs then run on autopilot until you turn them off and do so on a slow-drip message campaign to those users every minute or two so you stay inside the guidelines of YouTube and so that YouTube doesn't blacklist your channel.

Like all marketing campaigns it might take a little while to start seeing results but after a few weeks you'll start to see more comments on your videos and views. Also some more subscribers will begin following your channel. You can tweak your messages to change it up a bit if needed and measure your success right within their platform as well. My favorite thing about using this is that you don't need to sign in everyday and do this manually, it just runs for you and you can watch your channel grow. As people comment on your videos make sure you write back, thanking them for whatever they write or responding appropriately. Also, don't forget to ask everyone to sign up for your email list. Make it as easy as possible, provide a link to sign up and an offer with the link. Here's an example of a quick reply:

User1234: Thanks for sharing I love the video

You (response): Glad you like the tune User1234, here's a link if you want a free download of this song and the rest of the album. (link)

Notice I kept it short on the comment because they were fairly short, you want to make sure you're always responding appropriately to them. Do not overwhelm them with information or too long of a message back because you'll look desperate or seem annoying. Here's an example of a longer comment and a longer response.

User1234: Wow!! Thanks for the share, I didn't expect to get such a great song from your random message but this blew me away. I love the video and the song…I recently moved to a new city and can relate to the lyrics about moving away from home.

You (response): I'm glad you like the song User1234, where did you move to? I wrote this when I moved out to California and was having a difficult time. Here's a link if you want a free download of this song and the rest of the album.

In that comment you can respond and go a little more in depth, always ask a question to continue the conversation as well. This will keep them more engaged and mean more personally. For all your social media responses as well as emails it's good to add a question that elicits a response. Make sure to respond to their answers as well after you ask somebody something so they know you cared and you read it. For you it might just be another one of the thousands of people responding but for them it could be their one interaction with a band they love and go on to tell all their friends about.

As you can see, the key to all of this is that you're actually getting eyes and ears on your video. It's not just made up numbers or 5 second views of your song. Five real listeners hearing and responding to your song will go farther than 1 million purchased fake views or advertisements people are forced to watch. Once you get them to your video remember that this is a filter to capture their email address so you can continue marketing to them outside of YouTube.

If you're not familiar with YouTube's other features I suggest playing around with them a little bit as they can also get you traction. Annotations are the little text bubbles with links or "click me for more" buttons that pop up while you're watching a video. Unfortunately you can't link out to external website from these annotations but you can link people to other videos or tell them to subscribe for more. Remember that a subscriber on YouTube is good but it's just a borrowed fan, if YouTube changes policies or suddenly everybody jumps to the next great video sharing service you would lose them all. A better solution is to get somebody that watches your video and likes the music to sign up for your email list in exchange for a download of your album. I use an annotation on my videos that simply says "like this song? Download it for free in the link below". I paste a shortened custom link using smart.url or bit.ly with something like bit.ly/freedownloadSongTitle and that leads people to sign up capture page where they enter their first and last name in exchange for the download (see Chapter 5 for how to set this up).

Chapter 11 - Facebook

"Facebook was not originally created to be a company. It was built to accomplish a social mission - to make the world more open and connected." - Mark Zuckerberg

Facebook is the platform you're likely most familiar with. With over 1.86 Billion active users (as of 4th quarter 2016) and growing - that's nearly a quarter of the entire world population currently on Facebook. From your little sister to your grandma, nearly everybody has found a reason to sign up and use Facebook to keep up with friends, the latest trends or news stories. Facebook works a little different than the other sites, they have put a great deal of effort into limiting the amount of "business" posts people see and the ability for a business to reach out directly to users. Facebook's big differentiator is their algorithm that shows people what they would be most interested in. Because of that, when you sign on to your personal account you're not inundated with fake messages, follows and comments from business pages. Also because of that, it makes Facebook a tougher way for you to reach out to new random people and get them hooked into your music - they need to "discover" you organically, in fact as a business page you're not even allowed to message your fans privately unless you are responding directly to a private message from them. That being said, Facebook can also be a place to reach your fans where they will pay the most attention since so many of them use Facebook throughout the day. Call this sad if you'd like but another thing about Facebook is that the number of likes you have on your Facebook band page is still a determining factor used by many in the industry from tour booking to festivals and management companies.

Getting started with your band page is easy and if you know how to set up a profile, you'll be able to quickly set up the band page. First choose a profile picture that features your face(s), when the post shows up in somebody's timeline and they see actual faces as the profile picture they're more likely to form a connection to you than if it's your band's symbol or a picture of some cool mountains you found online. As with all your pictures make it identifiable to your brand and your music. Don't have a picture of you smoking a cigarette by a train if you're a children's band. Next you'll choose your cover photo, this photo is a secondary photo you can use and it's an amazing way to promote whatever it is you are promoting at the time. If you have a new song out you can use the song's artwork and words like "new song 'Falling Down' out now on iTunes, Spotify and Amazon - Click Link in Bio For Free Download". Another example would be a cover photo with all your tour dates and the name of your tour on the top. When somebody clicks into your page this will be the first thing they see so you want to make it count, it shouldn't just be another picture of you.

Next you have the 'About Us' section. I think the best way to set this up is to make it as simple as possible, don't put a long form bio in there or tons of information about your new album. I use this as a simple conversation space to get sign-ups, here's an example of what I would fill out:

Genre: Blues/Rock

Influences: band 1, band 2, band 3

Story: Listen to our music and check out all our videos at (website link)

Join Our Email List for FREE TUNES: EmailList.Link

You can add a few more items if you have something specific that sticks out. Maybe you just won New Artist of the Year for your city and want to put that in there as an award or have a specific slogan or quote you think would work. The key is to keep it simple, nobody on Facebook wants to read your full bio, just get them to the good stuff and get them converted into a fan if they're looking at your bio section.

The next thing you're able to incorporate would be a bandsintown or songkick tab to your page. This has changed a lot as Facebook's terms/conditions change but you can have a sidebar that says "events" that is set up with your bandsintown or SongKick events page. It will automatically update with all your upcoming shows. This saves you time from having to list them and automatically will post reminders on your page when new shows are coming up for your fans. These are the only automatic posts you should allow on your page. Bandcamp also allows you to add a music tab to the page as well so people can stream your songs and check you out quickly. You can also have a signup tab from your MailChimp or other email accounts. Those tabs used to be much more useful and get clicked a lot but with new changes to Facebook they have become much less useful and the majority of new viewers will simply scroll down in your timeline to see your latest videos, pictures and posts.

Now it's time to start posting, the first post people will see is a "pinned post". In the top right of all your posts you can choose to pin a post. Since this is the first post people will see it should be something that coordinates with whatever you're promoting. This could be for a new song, new album, merchandise or a tour. Just remember this will likely be the first taste somebody gets of your band and your brand so give them something good...you're a musician so I would always recommend a great music video.

Your first 1000 likes. So you have your page created, you're ready to get things going but you have 2 likes from your mom, your dad and nobody else. How are you going to gain fans? Let me first say this, there are ways to buy page likes...don't do this. Not only are they not real fans and pointless to have, they actually make you look bad to anybody that looks at your page. Anybody can quickly tell that a page that has 20,000 fans and 2 likes on each post is fake. Your likes need to be organic and real for you to get things started. For this, there is no substitute for hard work. Facebook offers a way to invite your friends to like your page but the conversion on that can be pretty low, I definitely would recommend using that feature (which you can find in the setting area of your profile) but you can only use it once, so you should create a buzz first by doing a few other things. The best way to get a quick following is to personally message each friend you have on Facebook. Go through your friends list and get it into alphabetical order if you can (rules change all the time on how you can view your friends). Just find a way to list them out and click to send a message that you'll paste into each message and edit from there. If you're saying, "I won't message people I haven't talked to in years because that's awkward" then you have the wrong mindset about this or the wrong kind of friends. The number of conversions from a personal message to a page like are staggering, when I did this my percentage of messages to likes were around 90%. It took me about 4 hours cumulatively to do which I spread out over a few days so I didn't lose my mind. Look at your friend's list right now and take 90% of that number. I had 1950 friends so that meant 1755 new likes hit my page in a week from a few hours of work. If you have a band even better, you could quickly jump your number to 4000 likes immediately. Maybe you have a few close friends that would be willing to help with this effort and invite their friends too. I'm telling you, it's painstaking for a few hours but it really works. Here's an example message that I sent out to somebody I hadn't talked to in about 8 years, I got back a thumbs-up and he liked my page, which led to him then checking out my album from the page and then developing into a real fan.

hey man, I know this is a random message but I'm spending the morning trying to get all my Facebook friends to like my band's page. It might seem dumb but believe it or not, it actually goes a long way for us. Here's the link, if you want music from us or anything like that for free let me know too and I'll send it over. Thanks for the help, hope you're doing great! www.facebook.com/bandname

You can fill in the person's name or something else to make it feel more personalized where you want. Spend the time on this because it will pay off in the long-run. After you send out those messages I would wait a week and then you can use the "invite friends to this page" feature from your page where you just click a button to invite people. This can work as a good follow up for anybody that maybe didn't like the page or forgot when they read the message. If you've already done this or you have friends that like your page you can search in Facebook to filter out people that have already liked your page when you message them as well. You'll want to avoid sending that message to anybody that already likes you.

Contests on Facebook can be a good way to promote a show you have coming up. If you're running a contest make the prize something related to your band, usually merch and free tickets work great but you can get creative and have backstage hangouts, pizza parties, jam sessions or whatever you can think of in exchange for them to spread the word about whatever you're promoting. These can be complex or simple depending on what you're giving away and how big you are. I've created point-system contest where people need to share a post, like your page, follow you on Twitter and tag a friend to get full points. I've also made simple ones just through Facebook that just say this:

we're playing a show at House of Blues San Diego on September 9th. Share this video and tag three friends below in the comments you would go with for a chance to win an exclusive backstage experience with us, free merch packages and 4 free tickets, winner announced September 5th - ticket link: ticketlink.com

It's simple and gets people to share your post with their friends. I would include a short video with your music in the post as well so everybody that gets tagged or sees the shared post will get a sense of the type of music you are. It produces social proof as well for your brand, because somebody sees a friends posting about you they take a little more time to check you out. The number 1 way people get into new music is when they're shown an artist by a friend. The total cost to you for this would be a few shirts and some comp tickets but this can spread the news of your show to thousands that otherwise wouldn't have gone. You also provide the ticket link in case somebody wants to just buy the tickets or if they don't win and want to refer back to the post leading up to the show.

The content you post. When you're not promoting anything you can add all sorts of posts to Facebook. This defines your brand when somebody checks you out so you should make sure to have relevant and interesting things to make people want to follow you more. Video content is king of Facebook, far more people will see a video in a timeline since Facebook gives a higher weight to any post with a video. After video content you'll want to use photos in as many other posts as possible as they get shown to more people and get more reactions than just text posts. Be funny and be yourself when you're posting, stick to your brand when you do this as well. Don't just post random garbage because you think you need to post every day - make sure it's relevant or you'll lose fans.

Live video for musicians can be a very valuable asset. When you "go live" every one of your fans gets a notification that you are live so they can tune in. If they sign on after you finished your broadcast they get a notification that you "were live" so they can watch the video on-demand afterwards. When you're streaming live you can also take questions or interact with fans through the comments section as well which allows your fans to become more connected with you. I did a broadcast live from a rollercoaster, from practice space to show a new song, from the side of the stage during a show and even from the audience by handing my phone to a fan (it has to be somebody you know and trust with your phone obviously). We've also started debuting new videos and our albums via Facebook live by using OBS Studio.

OBS studio is an encoding software that's open-source and free. You can stream live from your computer to Facebook and rather than just using a camera it allows you to simply play back a video, share you screen or connect through a webcam. I actually created a full live video of our 10 song album with a visualizer and streamed all 40 minutes to Facebook live for the debut. It's hard to capture somebody's attention on Facebook and get enough time for a full album but the way we did it we had thousands of people tune in and stay for the full album, many more just watched a few songs and then went about their day. Those numbers tripled after the broadcast was done and people that weren't online were notified that we went live. As you can see this tool can be very useful, there are a few things to understand about videos though before you do this. Familiarize yourself with the Facebook live video setting and follow their instructions found here https://www.facebook.com/facebookmedia/get-started/live. Make sure you encode the video at a low enough bit-rate that it will not lag or delay when playing as well. Handbrake is a great tool for re-encoding a video at a lower bit-rate and OBS Studio allows you to change the settings you upload at. All these tools are free and easy to use once you familiarize yourself. If that's too hard your phone will definitely do the trick for most videos you would stream and you only have to click the "go live" button to make it work. It's definitely worth exploring and using though to reach more people.

Forward Looking Note: you can stream live to Instagram, YouTube and Twitter as well but the features/functionality aren't nearly as useful for musicians as Facebook. I imagine those services will catch up very quickly though.

Look for a new app or service to likely emerge that will allow you to stream to all of those platforms simultaneously and easily so you can reach people on whichever platform they use at the same time.

Facebook Advertising in a nutshell. Most businesses that advertise on Facebook have a quick way to measure whether a marketing campaign is working. You basically need to know how much money you are spending and how much are you making from that expense. For a traditional business that's selling a product. You can track how many clicks your advertisement gets, how many people visit your page and leave without purchasing, how many return to your page when they see a second advertisement and how people buy the product. There are entire courses you can take on advertising and spending money marketing through Facebook.

For a band how do you measure a successful marketing advertisement? Is it when you get 100 likes on a status? Is it when more people like your page? More video views? More people visiting your website? I've seen thousands of dollars spent on campaigns the yielded zero return financially by bands when the campaign is over. So what's the point of spending money at all on advertising? Well that's the exact question you need to ask yourself before you spend any money on advertising through Facebook, Google, Twitter or any other platform. Who's the last artist you got really into and discovered from a Facebook ad? First ask what you hope to gain out of the campaign and make sure you have a way to measure your results, also make sure your results are either going to earn direct income (like selling tickets or merch) or will earn more income in the future by gaining fans or influencers. The second campaign is much harder to define than the first.

I'll start with the first type of campaign, using advertisements to sell tickets or merchandise directly. This can be the simplest campaign you set up and track basic results. Here's what you'll need to run this:

- A Facebook Advertisers Account (set this up when you set up your page, just give them your payment information and you're good to go)
- Fans that are interested in purchasing tickets, merch or anything else you may be selling and that like your page
- A product to sell and a place to sell it and add promo codes or tracking pixels. This could be Eventbrite, Universe Shopify, Gum Road or plenty of others depending on what you're selling. See chapter 6 on building your website and merch store.

First you'll want to create your target audience. Don't use the simple tools that Facebook will offer when you click "boost post" underneath a status. Go to the Ads Manager in Facebook to create and refine your audience using all the tools Facebook has to offer. From there you can filter by age, sex, location, interests and even interactions the person has had with previous posts you've created. Define your audience as well as your possibly can. Create multiple audiences that are similar as well so you can test you campaign. If you're selling tickets to a show in Seattle you can create a few different target audiences to test how they are selling, try different age groups, different interests and filters to find out what works best before you really focus your budget towards the group that's purchasing the most from you. You can then replicate that from city to city, continue to always test though. It takes more time than just clicking "friends of friends" when you boost a post but if you act like a scientist with your marketing you will be able to create predictable results with your campaigns. Imagine going to a city and knowing if you spend $500 on a campaign that you'll sell $1000 worth of tickets. If you're selling merch you should think of it the same way but your target audience of course will be different, rather than focusing on a location you'll focus on buyers of your merchandise (or whatever else you're selling). Never forget to test and retest these audiences before you commit money towards a campaign.

The next piece you'll test will be the actual advertisement. This will also always be different and needs to be something you test extensively before committing a lot of budget towards. Here are some recommendations to think about while creating your actual campaign/creative:

- A great video will work best, a great image will be next and simple text will be the weakest advertisement. If you create a weak video though it will not work as well as a great image or even great text. Whatever you make must be done right if you want to make an impact.

- Have one simple CALL TO ACTION as part of your advertisement. This should usually be a link to click unless you're running a contest. Don't have one link for merch and another for tickets, focus your messaging.

- Be real in your verbiage. Don't copy another band or another ad you've seen, be yourself and you'll sell yourself best. Everybody knows when they're being sold to or marketed at, it's why we fast-forward through TV commercials and click "skip ad" on YouTube. The best ads don't feel like ads at all, they connect with their audience and create an emotional response. A recent advertisement I saw simply said, "this ad cost us a lot, come see us live in San Diego", below that was a 30 second video clip of the best part of their new single and a ticket link. Being real will go farther than anything

- TEST, TEST, TEST. Create different versions of whatever you're doing so you can measure results and focus your money where it's working best.

- Create an emotional response with your advertisement. When somebody buys something on the spot it's 90% emotion. Think of it like this, when you're selling a ticket to a show you're actually selling an experience to somebody. And that experience is going to be different for every single person you sell to. Here are a few reasons why fans buy tickets to a show in no particular order:

1. To show a friend or a group of friends a good time

2. To connect with other people that like the same band they do
3. To scream out all the lyrics to their favorite song from the front row
4. To share a moment with their significant other
5. To say "I saw them before they got huge"
6. To connect with an artist that supports the same views they do

- Cater to your fan's emotions and you'll give them a reason to buy that ticket, t-shirt, hat, poster or album and they will thank you for the opportunity. In doing so you'll create a culture around your brand that fans appreciate and recognize. Jimmy Buffett is my favorite example of capitalizing off the emotions of a fan base. When you think of Jimmy Buffet, most likely you picture relaxing on a beach with drinks in your hand and no worries in the world. This is a perception he's created for his brand and despite having zero number-one hits, he continues to be one of the most successful touring artists in history. He has bars, restaurants, a wardrobe line, a line of beer and even a word that sums it all up: margaritaville.

- Make sure you can measure your results. If you can't see how many people bought a ticket because of your advertisement, your advertisement is pointless. Advertising is an **EXACT SCIENCE** and there is no room for guessing. A few simple ways you can do this is to create a few unique discount codes for tickets or merchandise depending on what ad they click on. The better and more accurate way though would involve Google

Analytics on your page and/or Facebook Pixels for tracking and remarketing.

- It takes 10 times before somebody buys. A rule of marketing is that you need to be in front of any prospect 10 times before you can expect them to buy or take interest in what you're selling. To do this you must be able to remarket to people that have clicked a link and didn't purchase so you can hit them again and again until they do. This takes an understanding of Facebook Pixels and Google Analytics so you can create goal-based campaigns. A goal-based campaign is another type of campaign you can set up in Facebook. It's more advanced but it takes into account the actual goal you want to accomplish. Rather than focusing on the number of clicks to your website you would focus on the number of times people click "confirm order" on the final order page after somebody has already entered their credit card information and shipping details. This means you're tracking every move from the first click to the last and analyzing data along the way.

So that's a lot of stuff for a simple marketing campaign right? Well here's the thing, you don't need to have all of that but it's critical to understand that this (and much much more) all exists when you're running your advertisement and spending your hard-earned money. Trust me when I say that the big labels understand all of this and have teams working to market, re-market, re-target and optimize campaigns. So when you click "friends of friends that like my page", set your budget for $100 and click submit I hope you know what you're up against with each dollar you spend. You're not just up against labels though and other musicians when you post something on Facebook, you're up against every single post out there. You have seconds to grab somebody attention to do whatever it is you want them to do and then you lose them to the next story.

I'm not going to dive more into everything you can do with Facebook, Google, Twitter or Instagram marketing here. That's another full book, course, maybe even years of research you can do on your own - in the same way I could spend chapters doing music theory as well but those books already exist and it just can't be summed up in a few pages so I'm not going to try. My true and honest advice is to learn this as well as you can and read a few other books on this subject before spending any money on it.

I know most of you aren't looking to become a master in marketing/advertising though so the other recommendation of course would be to find somebody that is great and offer a revenue split with them for selling tickets, merch or anything else that makes you money. This could be your marketing partner and could be profitable for both you and them. Typically this would be somebody that has plenty of experience with marketing but it also could be a fan or friend as well, if you can find an affiliate to do this you must ensure they can show actual result of sales made by them so you know they are not just taking ticket sales you would already have from fans. If done correctly this can be profitable both for you as well as them - create an agreement or contract that you will adhere to though and be detailed about what constitutes as payment for them and payment for you so there are no mistakes made, in this case being more detailed will save lots of time and hassle in the future.

I told you there were two ways you could use advertising, I just covered the first type where you're actually selling something people can buy immediately. The other way means you're not directly selling something but you're promoting a piece of your brand that will gain fans in the future or keep current fans more engaged. This can be music, a music video, an article about you, a blog post or a recent accolade. The reason you post just a song with no link to purchase or an article about you without anything else is simply to gain fans and because music, unlike other companies, must still remain cool. If somebody perceives any piece of you negatively (especially right off the bat) they will disregard you as a musician and it will be nearly impossible to get them to change their opinion. Basically you get one chance to form a new perception with somebody. Nobody likes to change their mind about something they've already decided on so if you screw up it will take A LOT to get them back.

Once you have that video, article, picture or whatever it is that you think people will like identify what your goal is. Do you want an email sign-up, a video view, and a "like" on your page or a comment on a status? How will you measure this and how will you target these people once you get whatever your desired result is. Facebook has made a very simple to define an audience based on people that taken action on a post such as people that have previously watched a percentage (whatever percentage you decide) of your video or people that have clicked on your image. Whatever you do decide, make it something that is meaningful and will be worth spending the money on so you turn them into a real fan later. Email, as always, is still king here if you're able to exchange a song download or something else for an email signup.

Boosting a post. If you're just going to boost a post you have the option of simply selecting "people that like your page and their friends". That can be the simplest way to get something out there to people if you're not actually selling something. Maybe you have a new music video or song to promote, this would be a good time to select that broad option to just get whatever that is in front of more people than it would normally get. Be careful though while doing this, those costs can all add up and remember you aren't seeing a direct return on that money spent. This option can be good to target around people that already like your page to let them know you have new content out so they can listen, share it themselves and show to friends and fall in love with you more. Just remember, who is the last favorite musician you found through a Facebook advertisement?

So if you take one thing from the advertising section for Facebook and other social media platforms I hope you understand that you should do your research before diving in and spending your hard-earned money on something that gets you nowhere. If you spend the time, do the research and test your campaigns you can see some real money and success from running advertising campaigns.

Chapter 12 - The Music Release

"My own saying is: 'create the hype, but don't ever believe it.'" - Simon Cowell

Once your social media accounts are up and you're gaining fans you're going to want to put out music...right, I mean we are musicians correct? How many bands in your hometown (maybe yourself included) have put out music that's better than everything on the radio right now but only received 50 plays on the song? You wrote the next Stairway to Heaven but you can't get anybody to listen to it, right? You just need one radio station to pick it up and play it once and you know it will get stuck in people's ears? Maybe you're waiting on your music video to "go viral". Well here's my theory on music releases and getting people to pay attention to your song, it's pretty simple. *Nobody is going to listen to your song until you shove it down their throats.*

Think about music on the radio right now. The average music listener turns on the radio and whatever is playing is what they listen to, that's how the majority of people still listen to music. Despite the existence of Spotify, Pandora, iTunes and the entire internet most people do not care enough on a regular basis to put on anything different. If they do go to Pandora or Spotify they're going to be listening to music playlists that are already made and catered towards what they like which is typically (you guessed it) what is also playing on the radio. That's because large record labels spend six to seven-figure budgets on world-wide exposure for a song. They do this because they understand that most people need music shoved down their throats before they decide they truly like a song.

Since you don't have commercial deals lined up already, world-tours and label money to play with you need to compete on your own level to break into as many people's ears as possible, a song "release" is the best way to do this because it's an event and a reason for you to blast them with the song as much as possible. How much is too much?

Well picture this scenario, there is one person that you need to listen to your song and like it. Your entire career relies on this one specific person hearing your song and getting into it. If this one person likes your song your life will be tremendously better and you'll reach all your highest goals. If that person doesn't listen to the song, you will lose everything, your life will go down the tubes and you'll be homeless within a week. Pretty extreme scenario I came up with, I know. So how would you reach this person? Would you send an email and hope it gets read? Would you post on Instagram because you know that person is there and might see your photo and click the link to download your music? Would you Tweet to that person's twitter handle with the link? Maybe you would send a text message with a download link?

If it was me in this scenario I would reach out as much as I possibly could as many ways as I possibly could WITHOUT BEING ANNOYING until that person listened to my song. The key-phrase is "without being annoying" in that sentence. If I emailed too many times I might get marked as spam; if I called too many times I may get my number blocked and I don't want that. You want to find the balance between the maximum amount of outreach and being annoying. You should think of your release the exact same way.

If you release a song it should be all you talk about for at least two weeks leading up to the release and all you talk about for at least 2-4 weeks after the release, add more time to these numbers if you're releasing a full album or EP. You should be hitting all of your social media campaigns with content, snippets, sneak peaks, behind the scenes, promo images, posters and live videos. You should email your list before its release, the day it's released and after the release with a review of the song from a blog or newspaper. Your top fans should be talking about it daily and be ready to share it as soon as it's released and the entire release should feel like an event. Don't be afraid to be persistent and post "too much" when you release new music just as long as you're not annoying them with it. Find that balance and live right at the edge of it. I got caught in the idea of "being cool" about releases and acting like it was no big deal when I put something out. I realized quickly that if I didn't care, nobody else would either.

Blogs, newspapers and magazines. I promise if you're just blasting your song out to a massive list of blogs, magazines and music reviewers that you're music is not going to be reviewed ever. I have run a music review site and never once reviewed a band based on a generic email sent to me with a link. I just had too many good bands to review and too much on my plate to even give them a listen. The artists that got a review reached out to me personally and developed a relationship - just like anything in life, a few emails back and forth getting me to talk a bit about the blog or telling me what they liked from my site went a very long way. After a bit of talking they would then inform me they were in a band and ASK if it would be alright to send music to listen to and maybe premiere on my site. They would let me know that if I ran a premier I would have an exclusive on the release for a week and all traffic would be led to my site from their fans, this of course is good for my site. Rather than a band asking me to do them a favor we've just conducted business and developed a relationship and usually they created a new fan in me. When they released their next song I of course was more than willing to help them out and suddenly they had one blog that was ready to post about them whenever they wanted.

This should be your strategy with music tastemakers. Develop relationships with them and continue those relationships so they will continue to write about you and share your music. That starts with being personal, understanding their blog, show, podcast, etc. and also making sure they cover your genre. Once you have a relationship built you can add them to a separate email list to follow up with them appropriately and easily when you have new releases. The more relationships you develop the more they will start to care about you as well, as more people are writing about you it becomes easier to get others to as well.

The email should contain everything they need to be able to write about your release as well. A good email will have the following information:

Intro Topic: The band ABC Band will be releasing their debut album titled "Best Album Ever" on December 3rd which will include their hit single "XYZ Song" which was featured last month as an iHeart Radio Top Rising Song.

Information about The Album/Song: This ten song album is a cohesive concept album with flowing music from the beginning to the end. The album is about the lead singer's battle he had with addiction when he was 19, every song on the album features other people that have struggled with addiction playing instruments or singing in the chorus sections. The final song is a tribute to his grandfather called "Going Home".

Link to Spotify

Link to iTunes

Link to YouTube

Link to SoundCloud

Link to Band Bio

Link to EPK

Link to Website

Contact Information

Finally you'll want to attach a few promo images for them to use as well. One image should be a clear high quality photo of you or your band and one other should be the album or song art-work. Before you're going to release your song about a month in advance you should reach out to these tastemakers to let them know about the release and try to line up one premiere and at least one other review.

If you're just getting started with reaching out to blogs I recommend looking at fluence.io and submithub.com. These are websites that allow you to pay for these tastemaker's time. A popular music journalist might charge $5 per minute to listen to songs, if your song is 4 minutes that means it will cost you $20 for them to listen to it. They do actually listen and provide feedback for your song but my suggestion is to understand a bit about them before you submit to make sure you're submitting to the right person with the right type of blog, just as if you were doing it for free. If your music is good, this is a great way to get coverage.

Finally you have fiverr.com as a last resort for getting reviews. Fiverr is a website where you pay $5 or more for various individual's online services. People can define whatever they will do for $5 and you pay through the system. If you type in "music review" on the website you'll see a bunch of people that will review your album and put it up on their music review blog. Because they review anybody that pays them money (usually between $5-$20) the music they review can be poor quality and lacks genre. Because of that few people typically read or follow their blog for new music. But getting a review on a website like this will give you a reason to tell people about your song again following the initial release and it will work to continue hype for the release and get somebody to click the link and actually give your song a listen.

This whole thing is all about hype. When your release date is lined up and you have the newspaper or blog lined up for press you can work out your hype schedule. I've found that about two weeks out is a good time to start to run promo for a new single and 3-4 weeks out is good for a new album. Get creative with this, you should have about 5-10 different pieces of creative content to put out leading up to each release. This can be behind the scenes recordings, sneak peaks, 5 minute video documentary about the album creation, 2 minute video about the making of the music video, album artwork, live video announcements or hidden message announcements (i.e.: big announcement tomorrow).

Make sure for the two weeks leading up to release you're blasting all the social networks with these and also sending at least one email out to your list to let them know about the new release.

On the actual release day you'll want to schedule everything to go out at the same time, you can track what time that should be based on your analytics for highest traffic and open rates. If you're not sure how to do that or don't want to I would say that 11am in your time zone is also always a pretty good bet when most people are on their computers.

I like to post a one minute video clip of the song on social networks to get people listening. If it's a music video that's perfect, just choose your favorite part and post that. If not, you'll need to create some sort of video as discussed in the video section. Video will spread much farther than just a link would so you need to line up with a lyrics video or live video of some sort when you make this. That one minute video is a teaser and then I put the link in the status so they can click to see more. If you have a blog or newspaper premiere you can link out to their page for people to hear the rest of it. This teaser video and link will go on all your social media sites. For your email campaign you will have a teaser image with a play button in the middle of it and just a short description that you've released a new song and you want your fans to listen. Ask them for feedback on it, tell them to reply to you. When they click the image it should have a hyperlink to automatically take them to the song.

In every part of the release you should have a way for people to download the song. This will be a link that will take them to your email sign-up page. If they are on your email fan list already you can use something like fangate or toneden.io to create a social media gate so they have to like your Facebook page to download. You can place this in the comments of your post, in your post, in the body of the email or the description information on YouTube. Wherever you feel it looks best and is most appropriate. Make it easy to see and bold, many fans will share your song if you do this right so you want to capture those new fans as much as possible.

If you have the funds you can also boost your release as well. This is the reason you play music so you want to spread it as much as possible. Instagram, Facebook and Twitter can all be great places to promote a post but I would suggest limiting your spend to fans and friends of fans to maximize your reach and ensure you're targeting the right people. There's no correct formula for this since you realistically aren't going to see a direct return from any money spent here, the goal would be to simply get as many plays as possible on your video to capture new fans and spread your brand for future shows, merchandise and other money making opportunities. I talked about this before but what is the last artist you've gotten into off of a Facebook ad for their new single? I think Facebook ads can be a great way to get current fans into your new release but it can be tough to generate a new fan off a social media advertisement. Music just doesn't connect that way.

You should time out your releases so you can continue building hype off each release. Typically you want to be releasing singles every 4-8 weeks. If you are releasing an album you want to strive to record and put out a new album every 6-8 months with singles in-between to promote the album and build hype. If you do this correctly you will continue to build upon previous releases and the hype for your next release will grow from the one before it, your audience will be continually engaged and awaiting your next big music release rather than forgetting about you.

Chapter 13 - Albums, Singles and EPs

"I've basically got an album full of singles." - Coolio

You've probably heard "the album is dead" lately from pretty much everywhere. This can be true for some genres and not true for others. To keep it very simple I say this: regardless of your genre, if you have enough music and a message that needs to be delivered in the form of an album, you should release an album. Make sure you have a good reason for releasing your music as an album, there really is no need to create albums anymore unless there is a message or story to tell and you need multiple songs to deliver that message. Just grouping 10 songs together because you think you need an album is not a good reason.

From a marketing perspective singles are much better. It's easier for an average passive listener to absorb because it only takes 4 minutes of their time to listen to. Releasing 10 singles allows you to build hype 10 times over the course of 10 months where an album release only gives you one large release. So if you are putting out an album the more single releases you can get out of it, the better. On a 10 track album you might have 4 or 5 releases leading up to the album release. This can give you 5-6 months of content while you write, record and get ready to release the singles from your next album. The writing and recording process should be on-going.

Your obvious "in-between" would be the EP. At 4-6 songs it's far easier to record and produce than an album but carries a bit more artistic value than just a single. I would select 1-3 singles to release leading up to the release of the EP. You can also always add 4-6 more songs to an EP and turn it into a full length album later on if you wanted to.

Basically there is no right or wrong way to release music nowadays so I don't like to hear "the album is dead". There are only wrong ways to release and market an album.

Chapter 14 - Booking Shows

When you're onstage and the audience is smiling and singing and bopping along and you're all on the same level, it's the best feeling in the world. It may sound dumb and corny to say it, but it's like pure love." Joan Jett

Finally we're getting to the fun stuff, the greatest moments in a musician's life are had up on the stage playing for fans. Without the last chapters (and a few more coming up) you might as well just keep playing in your garage though for your dog and your parents. To book a show you need to have fans and to get fans you need to engage and be able to market yourself.

Here are a few basics about booking shows, whether you're booking a local gig or a national tour...the same fundamentals will apply.

- It's all about relationships, the better your relationship is with the booker the easier it will be to get booked
- Focus on what you can do for them, not what they will do for you.
- At the end of the day, all they want to know is that you will bring enough people to the show. Their job is to fill the venue, they aren't interested in cool

sounding music playing to an empty bar (unless you're booking a cover gig and don't need to promote).

- Regardless of how long it takes them to get back to you, get back to them as soon as possible. Sometimes it takes weeks or months for a booker to finally listen to what you sent, you want to respond back to them when you're still on their mind so they don't forget about you.
- Make it as easy as possible to book you. Give them the following in your email:

  - Who you are
  - Where you're from
  - What you sound like
  - Accolades
  - Expected Draw (back up with proof if possible)
  - Link to LIVE video
  - Link to Socials
  - Link to Website
  - Contact Information

- If you do everything right you will likely get about 30 seconds of their attention to watch the video of you playing live. This should be a great video with quality sound and stage presence. A great live video will change your booking experience in a huge way.
- Stay organized, know who you contacted and know when to reach back out

Chapter 15 - Booking Your First Local Gig

"Why don't venues get back to you? Because they're busy." - Dave Ruch, (performer and teaching artist)

I shouldn't have to say this but make sure you can play a quality set and you're well-rehearsed at this point. I wish I didn't have to say that but I've seen enough local bands to know how many get up on stage unprepared, your show is one of the most lasting impressions you can make on anybody whether they're friends, family members, co-workers or fans that found you online. Don't disappoint them when they come to see you live.

Once you're ready to start playing some shows you should identify where you would like to play. You have two options when you decide to play a show, you can headline the night or you can support a headlining act.

First figure out what your draw will be, this is a guess (especially for your first show) but try to be analytical about this and figure out who will really come out to support your show. If it's your first show this will likely be friends and family. Let's say that number is 40 people. Now you decide on whether you're going to be direct support for a larger band at a bigger venue or if you want to headline the night at a smaller venue. Here's an equation you can use for booking pretty much anywhere at any time.

- **Headliner - Your draw should be equal to or slightly less than the venue's capacity**

- **Direct Support - Your draw should be at least 15% of the venue's capacity.**

So if your draw is only 40 you can look for small venues that hold about 40-50 people. This could be tiny bars, coffee shops, house parties or small acoustic stages. The idea is for the room to feel packed, like you had a great showing regardless of how big your audience is. Being at a packed house show in a small venue makes an audience member feel important, like they got into a show that's a really big deal. The crowd has more fun, pays more attention and is much more likely to spread the word, come to another show and buy merchandise/support you in future endeavors. Fifty people in a fifty person venue feels like a massive success, fifty people in a 300 person venue feels like a completely dead show, nobody likes to go there. You've probably gone out to support a friend at a show and nobody is there, it's not fun...it's awkward. Don't get starry eyed by the idea of playing in a big popular venue with name recognition, stick to the formula.

If you're looking to play direct support this can be a great way to get in front of a bigger band's audience. Using the formula for a support band, if your draw is about 40 you can look to play in a 250+ person venue. Bigger bands coming through town look for smaller bands to play on the lineup that can fill a buffer and bring people out, their magic number is typically about 15% of the venues capacity. This is a great way to get your live act up in front of lots of new people from your hometown. You want to make sure before you agree to one of these shows that the headliner is not making a booking mistake and that they will actually bring out enough people to fill the place.

So now that you've identified where you want to play you should take those spots and put them into a spreadsheet. List the sheet out with columns

- Venue Name
- Booking Contact
- Phone
- Email
- Tentative Dates
- Notes / Next Steps

Now is the "fun" part of booking. You're going to call all of these places directly and ask whoever picks up to talk to the person that handles booking. Make sure you have a calendar with open dates in front of you and make sure you have your pitch down for the night. You'll want to let them know what your sound is like, what your draw will be and you should have an idea of what you would want for compensation. It's rare that you'll get on the phone with whoever is in charge of booking but in case you do, you don't want to be fumbling your words and caught off-guard.

The typical response you'll be told is that the person in charge of booking is not in. Usually that person will tell you to email their booking address with your information for all booking inquiries. Get the name of the booker and the booking email address. For that email I've found that being slightly informal and to the point works better, bookers are usually easy-going and receive a lot of emails. They want to move fast through bands they like so make their job as easy as possible. Here is an example of a good outreach email.

SUBJECT: (band name) to play May 6th

hey (booker name), I was given your information about booking at (venue). We're a local group and frequent (venue name) all the time for shows. Our sound is a mix of classic-rock with indie-electronic we sound a bit like Jack White meets Alt-J. Here's a video of us playing live last month to get an idea of our sound: LINK

Anyways, we're looking to play there on May 6th or the 13th if that's open but have some other dates open as well. We expect to bring about 50 people out for the show and have an acoustic opener that will bring another 20 or so.

Check us out and let me know.

NAME

PHONE

EMAIL

WEBSITE

I got out all the needed information about our music genre, our draw, the date we had in mind and gave a link to a video of us playing live. Don't leave the dates up to them and ask if anything is open, of course dates are open at some point in the future. Give the booker a date you want and start the conversation.

It takes bookers a while to get through things. I usually give it 4-5 days before following up. If you can find the booker's number that's always a plus but if you have to email them again you should reply to your last email so everything you previously wrote is below and keep the "RE:" in the subject, studies show much higher open rates of emails with RE: in the subject. I usually just say something like this:

Hey (booker), just following up from my email last week. We'd love to put on a great show there so hoping to hear back on that date or possibly others. You can check us out again at LINK.

NAME

PHONE

EMAIL

WEBSITE

You can keep sending variations of that follow up email until you hear back. Persistence pays off and assuming you have a great show once you do finally get booked, you will be in from then on at that venue. Again, bookers at these local venues are looking to do one thing. They want to put asses in seats at the bar and get people through the door. They don't care about your sound as much as they care about your draw, prove you can bring a crowd and you'll get booked.

Chapter 16 - Promoting Your Shows and Playing the Right Amount

"A concert is not a live rendition of our album. It's a theatrical event." - Freddie Mercury

Once you're able to get booked locally you need to make sure you don't over book in your hometown. For some bands this concept can be very difficult. Think of it like this, if your favorite band came to town to play shows how many times would you see them? Would you go twice? Would you go a third time in a month? How about 20 times? No matter how good you are, your fans don't want to see you all the time.

What starts to happen is that fans say, "I'll just catch the next one" and you begin to lose audience at your shows, essentially you're competing with yourself for your own fans. Audiences start to die down at shows and things fizzle out. To prevent this from happening, you can limit the number of big shows you promote to about 4-6 per year per city. This doesn't mean you can't play more shows, just don't promote them. You should be clear and upfront with somebody that books you to let them know whether this is or isn't a show you will be promoting so you're both on the same page and have the same expectations going into the show. By spreading out the big shows you promote by about three months you'll give yourself a chance to build up buzz and anticipation. Your fans won't say, "I'll just hit the next one" because they will have to wait a long time to make that one happen.

Each show should be a unique and a fun experience for your audience. You're competing against literally everything somebody can do on a Friday or Saturday night so you want this to be something your fans look forward to and have fun at. If a fan misses a show they should feel like they missed out on a once in a lifetime experience, even if you're going to be playing again in a few months. To create a unique experience you should be thinking outside the box, here are some ideas I've seen with success to turn your show into a unique experience:

- Create a festival with other local bands
- Bring in local vendors to sell items at your show
- Free happy hour party before at a friend's house
- CD Release Party
- Charity Partnership
- Tailgate Party
- Dance Group
- Cook-off beforehand
- Theme Party
- Clothes/Toys Donation
- Yoga with music

There are so many different ideas you can do, find something that fits the message of your brand and work with that. You will have to be creative and it will take planning but you need to keep your show entertaining to keep people coming and enjoying their experience.

You will want to give yourself at least a month of promotion time for the show. When you announce the show if you're able to sell a limited amount of discounted presale tickets you should have that link ready to send. You would ideally put out an email, an announcement on all your social feeds, songkick or bandsintown and also set up a Facebook event to invite friends and fans to. You should also have the poster/artwork for all social media spaces to have continuous promotion of the show. If you have a video for the show you can release that as well. The social media campaign can be slow but get more and more consistent as the event comes closer. In the last week leading up to the show you should be posting a few times a day about the show to get the hype up, this should include pictures, posts, live videos and more. The final piece would be to put together a text-message list of friends that you can quickly reach, you can use an app like "HeyYou" to reach out via text message in the masses without seeming like you're sending a spammy group message. When it comes to selling tickets I don't think you can do too much promotion nowadays, just stay within the constructs of your brand when you do it so it doesn't seem uncool.

The best way to sell tickets is going to be word of mouth so you want to target the fans that have already bought tickets to really get them to promote the show themselves. You can make offers to people that already purchased to buy additional discounted tickets or if you want to get creative, you can create a referral link for each ticket sold, put something like, "want this ticket for free? Refer this show to three friends and we'll hook up your ticket". Those people are already going to the show so why would they not want to tell their friends about it and get more people to go with them.

Since each show will be special you should find reasons why your local papers would want to talk about it. You should put out a press release and send them to music bloggers in the local scene as well as newspapers and magazines. You'll want to give them notice about the show, typically about 6-8 weeks is what a print magazine would need to get your show date and article into a publication. Make sure you give them enough time to discuss the article and get it approved for the next month's magazine. More importantly, you need to give them a *reason* to print the article. The first newspaper writer I ever met told me he starts off every article with "the world is going to end", and then he works back from there (not literally those words but you get the idea). Your press release needs to have that same zing behind it, what is the reason anybody should care about your show? What will make you stand out from all the other shows going on that weekend? Be creative and find a reason to stand out from the noise.

The final piece of promoting your show comes from the show itself. Make sure your audience has a phenomenal time at the show. Make it an experience they will tell all their friends about. Meet with them after the show and talk to your fans, get to know them and make them feel good about who you are. Sign them up on your email list and keep it organized so you can follow up with them later. Promotion for your next show starts as soon as you get off the stage, it's the best time to lock in new fans for life so take advantage of this time and don't just go sit in the green room by yourself with a beer.

Chapter 17 - Touring Musicians

"You know, when you really connect with the instrument and everything just comes out on an emotional level very naturally through your playing. That's, you know, a great night. And I think the reason I love touring so much is you're chasing that high around all the time, trying to have another good night." Slash

How do you avoid overplaying your hometown but still promote and play large shows more often? Start touring. For most musicians touring is actually more than just being on the road and playing shows. It's a goal, a lifestyle, a rite of passage, a dream for some. For some it's what they said when they were 10 years old about what they want to be when they grow up, "a musician that travels all around the world playing shows". For others, touring is a necessary evil that comes with success in the music business. Whatever you think about touring, at some point this is going to come up.

If your music is good and people are responding to it they are going to want to see you live when you come to town. If you've been doing your job marketing you should have some sort of a following in the cities you're going to travel to for shows. This is important, if you don't know you have fans in a city you probably shouldn't be playing there yet. If your live show is tight and you're running every piece of it correctly, a tour is a way to turn casual fans of your music into die-hard super fans for life.

I've seen tours personally on both extreme ends of the spectrum. Some tours launch a band from local band status to national acts with thousands of fans. I've seen the other end of the spectrum as well, a band going on a 10 week tour playing for nobody in each city, gaining zero fans, not selling merch and coming back broke at the end of it with nothing gained. Touring is not a complicated concept to master but it all boils down to one very important question, why are you touring? You need to ask yourself before you go on tour why you are booking a tour and be very honest with yourself. Many bands/artists fall into what I call the "vanity tour". A vanity tour allows bands to say things like, "yeah we just got done with a 6 week tour" or "we just played 20 cities last month". Sometimes bands go on a vanity tour because they have a desire to travel, sometimes it's because it's what they think they're supposed to do, sometimes it's just to tell their parents how great the band is doing. Whatever the purpose is of a vanity tour, it's not the right way to tour and it's not the right reasons for touring.

Your reason for touring will not be vanity. Your purpose for touring may vary but in general the reason for booking a tour should be to gain as many possible fans in new cities while simultaneously earning money through ticket sales, merchandise sales and any other revenue streams you can create while on the road. Remember, if you can only play four big shows in your hometown per year that means you need to play in another city if you want to play up to eight big shows per year. If you add another city into the mix you can play up to twelve shows now, and so on. It's incredibly important to think about your tour like this before you even talk about where you're going to play.

Chapter 18 - Booking Your First Tour

Cold calling is about developing social skills and getting used to rejection. We are constantly selling something to somebody. Shahid Khan

Okay, we have a great band and an awesome local following. We're ready to start playing in other cities, create die-hard fans and earning more money. Why aren't all the cities calling us yet and asking us to play? How do we jump on tour with a huge band and get all their fans to like us?

Just like pretty much everything in music, it takes time but most importantly it takes fans to make all that happen. If you're about to tour for the first time you're going to learn lessons on the road and you're going to understand what it really takes very quickly. But the reason you're reading this book is to save yourself from the lessons you have to learn on the road so I'll save you some hardships and hard-knock lessons life taught me so you don't make the same mistakes.

You're climbing up a mountain, just start with the first step and take it from there. In most cases I suggest doing your own booking to start and then once you get a good understanding of how it works hiring a booking agent or manager to handle booking. Personally, I think booking a tour is awful, it's a lot of phone calls/emails with no returns or late replies, it's scheduling and coordinating with multiple bands in multiple cities and it takes a lot of hard and very draining work. The process of booking in different cities is not different from booking in your hometown at venues but the only difference is that it's harder to prove to a booker that you're going to bring people to the show since you're not from that city. I don't need to re-write how you're supposed to book at venues (see Chapters 13 and 14 for a refresher). The biggest asset you can have for booking in other cities is "proof" of your following in that city. If you can bring out 50 people to their venue you need to be able to explain how/why this is going to happen. If you've played in that city before that easy, you can just show them your sales for the last show. If this is your first time you'll have to be more creative. Here are a few ways to show that to a booker that work:

- Show fan data from your socials, email list, etc. that proves you have a following in that city
- If somebody from the band used to live in that city you can tell a story to explain why you'll have such a big following. Example: "we know this is our first time in (city) but our drummer just graduated from college there and was in a fraternity, he has a group of about 50 people that will definitely come out to support".
- Talk about how you will be promoting. Radio, newspaper, social media, PR, etc.
- When all else fails, you can make things up...I've gotten plenty of first time gigs by simply stating I've

played in that city before and brought out XX number of people. Usually a booker won't check up on what you send them, but you will definitely have to work your butt off to make sure you bring a crowd. If you know you're going to bring a big crowd this is fine, it's a lie that hurts nobody...if you don't think you can realistically bring the number you say though you'll have karma working against you. If karma isn't enough to scare you you'll also have a pissed off booker that could tell all the other bookers in the area about your band.

This is booking for the club shows though and there are plenty of other shows you can play on the road. The best thing you can do for money while you're touring is to find some big paying shows while you're on the road that you can play interlaced with the club/bar shows. These big paying gigs sometimes are called anchor shows or anchor dates. Many times you'll get a few of these first and book a tour around them. These could be wedding gigs, college shows, corporate parties, birthday parties or anything else like that. These are the shows that pay a few thousand dollars for you to play so just a few of these can completely change the financial outcome of your tour as you can see.

Depending on your music type, whether you're a solo artist or band, if you play covers and other factors you'll have to find what works best for you. Here are just a few great resources to start with when hunting for these.

GigMasters.com - This is great for both solo artists and bands. As this is written they currently still offer a 30 day free trial. After that, costs vary depending on distances you want to receive leads for and how many categories you would like to be listed under. Basically GigMasters sends you leads for shows that match your criteria and allows you to send a quote for your services to the client. If you give them a "yes" response to their gig request you will see their number and email. I can't stress this enough, call them and email them to talk as soon as you can if you want to play the gig. If you're friendly, professional and personable they will likely go with the first person they speak with that fits their budget. Ask them if they know what they want to spend, let them give you a number first. You might know you'll play for $500 but let them tell you $2500 is their budget first before your give them a quote. Don't under-value yourself.

Colleges are another source of big paying gigs that can make or break your tour. Getting these gigs involve going through either NACA (National Association Campus Activities) or APCA (Association for Promotion Campus Acitivies). They run regional conferences for college campus activities board members to meet and find the talent they are going to book for the upcoming year. These are typically college juniors and seniors that are given large budgets to work with for booking everything from bands to magicians to hypnotists for the upcoming school year. You as an artist have the option of buying your way into these conference to perform for these college decision makers. If you are able to perform at the conference (and you're good enough) the chances are very likely that you're going to get booked for shows. Beyond that, the colleges will actually meet to schedule out your tour for you. If you say that you're going rate is $3,000 a show, you might also say that if you get booked for 5 shows at once you'll do each one for $2,200 per show. This entices the colleges to work together around your booking dates to make an offer of $11,000 and they'll work the dates out to make sure you can drive from one to the other with reasonable time.

Before you jump on your computer and start trying to sign up there are a few things to understand first. Number one I highly recommend you work with a college booking agent to secure your NACA performance. They don't just take anybody to perform and these conferences, you need to submit a demo and also a live video recording to get a chance to perform. You also want to come in prepared with dates, merchandise/stickers for your booth, business cards and most of all you should be ready to play. An agent will save you a lot of time and also a lot potentially wasted money in applying or buying a spot at a conference which costs thousands and result in you not getting booked by anybody.

Another thing about the college gigs, these can be very weird shows. That doesn't mean they won't be worth playing - they will pay a lot of money - but they aren't necessarily going to advance your career in huge ways. Sometimes you might be playing a festival outside and have hundreds of people loving your music. Other times you might be in the corner of the dorm cafeteria playing through one tiny speaker. Whatever the gig is, you show up and give your best performance, get your check and move on.

College/corporate/wedding/party shows - these dates are a starting point for a tour and can be your insurance to make sure you're making money when you hit the road. If you line up 3-5 of these shows you might hit the road knowing you'll make about $4,000-$8,000 over a few weeks rather than blindly crossing your fingers and hoping to make money on the road. These shows should be accompanied by club shows. If you book a college show at University of Illinois you should also be looking to play a club show that night around Champagne. Don't rest on one of these shows and think that's all you should be doing in that city. The people that come to those corporate or college shows are not likely to see you next time you're in town, they're going to a free hot-dog lunch for incoming freshman or the sales kickoff meeting their company is making them attend, you just happen to be playing music there as well. Remember why you're on the tour, it's to gain real ticket-buying, music-listening fans and continue building a hardcore audience in that city.

Chapter 19 - Making More Money on the Road

"Cash is oxygen." - Gary Vaynerchuk (entrepreneur / social media guru)

Especially for your first tour, you should find other ways you can make money on the road to support what you're doing. If you can work from the road this is ideal, many positions now are virtual - this means you can do your work from anywhere and get paid for a job while you're touring around playing shows. If you have a skill or trade that allows you to do this you're in a very good place as a musician. This doesn't mean it's the only way to make money on the road though outside of the shows.

First, as a band you need to understand how much more money merchandise sales can make you. You should have merchandise ranging from the $5 range to the $50+ range for everybody that wants to buy a memento and also contribute to your band. A recent example, I was playing a show at the top of a ski lodge in the mountains. The show paid $1,500 a day for 4 days. The first day we left our merchandise in our condo on accident, we sold no merchandise and received no tips for the first show - nobody even knew they were supposed to buy anything from us or tip us because we didn't put out a tip jar. The next day we didn't make that mistake again, we cleared $350 in sales, since we have large mark-ups on our merchandise we made about $270 profit from those sales. The next day was a Saturday and was even bigger sales and Sunday did just as well. This is a lot of extra money for just selling merchandise at your shows. You can see how that can add up quickly over the life of a tour to cover expenses. Really hone in on your merch table and test what sells the best, ditch the items that take up room and don't sell.

Another money earning technique for some artists would be house-shows. You can offer personal house shows or living rooms acoustic shows for fans. It's the ultimate experience. Pitch it like this:

On a very limited basis we're offering an ultimate (band name) experience. We will set up and play a show for you and your friends live in your living room (or anywhere you'd like us to play). There is a per event price of $_____ to play this show which is way less than our normal rate but still covers all our gas and expenses to get there. Message us directly at (email) and we'll give you all the details.

These shows have been some of the most rewarding shows I've played and the experience people get is something they typically will remember forever. I had somebody come up to me years later and tell me he saw my band playing a private show at south by southwest in a house and he still tells people about it today. For me it was just another show in a cramped living room, for the 30 people in the audience though it was the chance of a lifetime. When you follow up with details you can also ask if they have a place for you to crash as well, make sure it doesn't seem like you're pressuring them to crash on their couch but some people will be incredibly inviting once you reach out.

Other ways you can make money:

- Music lessons via skype
- Search Craigslist/Postlets in the city you're in for gigs
- Drive Uber/Lyft during downtime in new cities
- Ask local restaurants about acoustic gigs
- Check apps like GigTown for last minute gigs in cities you're in
- Find freelance online projects you can do virtually (use upwork.com or guru.com)
- Look into a credit card that pays back larger amounts on gas purchases. If you get 5% back on gas vs. paying cash, over the course of a tour you can save hundreds of dollars.

Chapter 20 - Crowdfunding

"Crowdfunding isn't about collecting money. It's about making something happen with a crowd of people who believe in something." - *Jozefien Daelemans (entrepreneur, blogger, writer)*

If you are trying to avoid any sort of crowd-funding because of your own personal ideals and feelings about crowd-funding projects in general than you can skip this chapter but you should also know you're leaving a lot of money on the table. Over $30,000 **per creation** is what Amanda Palmer is paid off of Patreon. My friend's band, I Fight Dragons, recently made over $130,000 from one Kickstarter campaign. Countless musicians are making thousands of dollars per month from Patreon backers and thousands of bands have completely funded projects that would have cost thousands by launching them on Kickstarter or IndieGogo.

Kickstarter and IndieGogo are traditional crowd-funding platforms. If you don't know how they work, an artist will set up a project and a goal amount of money they need to raise for the project to happen. If you donate to the project you will receive rewards based on different reward tiers; the more you donate, the better the rewards get. For kickstarter, if the creator does not reach their goal, the project doesn't happen and nobody that backed the project gets charged. For IndieGogo the project does not have to meet the final goal, everybody is charged automatically. These platforms are changing constantly so you'll definitely want to check for the latest on how they work.

Patreon is a little different, instead of asking for one big donation to reach a goal, Patreon is broken up into either monthly, bi-weekly or "per-creation" based funding. So for a musician this means that instead of raising $10,000 all at once to fund an album and then delivering rewards, you would likely receive a lower amount but it would be paid to you monthly or every time you released a new song.

Each platform has its pros and cons, there is a lot of research and studies you can do on these but a few points that you need to consider when you set this up:

- Make sure you're giving people something they want. This isn't a handout club, think to yourself, "would I back for this amount to receive this." If you're asking for $50 to receive a tank-top you're running a handout club and this might affect the number of donations you receive.
- On the other hand make sure you don't underprice your rewards. If you give people a premium t-shirt for a $5 donation you might get thousands in donations but you'll spend more on fulfillment and won't make any money (and might even lose money).

- Don't let the video hold up your launch. Too many people get stuck on the video, you don't need to hire a professional to create the video for your Kickstarter. You're musicians and you're creative so come up with something cool on your own, filming with an iPhone is perfectly fine. If you're running a Kickstarter to raise $50,000 for a new drone that follows your skateboard you should spend thousands on your video. You don't need to follow what they do though, keep it simple and get it done.
- Include pictures of the merchandise or rewards.
- Make the page simple to read and understand, test this on friends or family to make sure they get it as well.
- Get creative with your rewards. The best rewards are the ones that ideally cost you nothing to make. A skype call or a lunch date are great ways to get money at zero cost.
- Create a way for big donations. You have good friends, family and people that want to see you succeed. Give them a way to back you at the amount they want. So many friends gave me $200 during the last Kickstarter it blew my mind. The reward tier I first thought of as a joke at $1,500 filled up by the end of the campaign as well. Never underestimate what people are willing to give, if you leave the rewards low you'll receive low donations only.
- Calculate all of your expenses before making your prices. Do the math and understand how the prices will change as you scale up. Don't forget shipping.
- Fulfill your backers and keep them updated. This is a great way to form a personal relationship with

them, regardless of the type of crowd-funding campaign you're running you can stay in touch and let them know as you complete more of your project, as you hit stumbling blocks, funny stories from the road. Never forget that they gave to you so you could follow your dreams.

Chapter 21 - In Closing

Did I cover every single thing you're going to come up against in this book? No, I know that I didn't – I wish that I could. There's just too many things that can happen in this business and I wanted to focus on the things that I know well. You might be asking, "Why didn't you write about getting signed by a label"? Well it's because I honestly don't know anything about that other than what I've read in books because I've never signed with a label before. My advice wouldn't be first hand and there are plenty of good books out there that can offer more advice for that type of stuff. I wanted to stick to what I know, in the future if I sign on with a big (or small) label I will let you know what that experience teaches me and possibly release an updated version of this book with the all the latest and greatest things I've come up again.

Please understand this book should be used as guidelines to form your music business and start generating money but it is not the only way to do things or a road map that will work 100% of the time. It is designed to make you work smarter but smart work will never replace hard work in this industry...it can only supplement it. Good old fashioned door-to-door grassroots marketing will always go far (whether that's literally door-to-door or virtually).

Many of the websites and apps I named are probably gone by the time you're reading this. There's nothing I can do about that, it's literally how fast the industry changes. I promise there is another app that does the same thing out there, you just need to research and find it. Remember, it's not important which vehicle you use to accomplish the task, it's just important that the task gets done.

Please reach out to me as well if you have questions or want to connect. My personal email address is bradalansweet@gmail.com and I would love to hear your feedback. Good luck and I truly hope this has helped you to spread your passion to the world and make more money while doing it.

If you enjoyed this book, I would love it if you left a quick review at the reseller of your choice. It helps tons and it can help others to learn more as well. Thanks!

- **Brad**

Made in the USA
Lexington, KY
14 February 2019